The *Bird Lover's* GARDEN

Margaret MacAvoy and Pat Kite

FRIEDMAN/FAIRFAX
PUBLISHERS

A FRIEDMAN/FAIRFAX BOOK

©2000 by Michael Friedman Publishing Group, Inc.

Library of Congress Cataloging-in-Publication data available upon request.

ISBN 1-56799-727-9

Editor: Susan Lauzau
Art Director: Jeff Batzli
Designer: John Marius
Production Manager: Richela Fabian

Color separations by Colourscan Overseas Co Pte Ltd
Printed in China by Leefung-Asco Printers Ltd.

1 3 5 7 9 10 8 6 4 2

For bulk purchases and special sales, please contact:
Friedman/Fairfax Publishers
Attention: Sales Department
15 West 26th Street
New York, New York 10010
212/685-6610   FAX 212/685-1307

Visit our website:
www.metrobooks.com

Now the summer came to pass
  And flowers through the grass
Joyously sprang,
  While all the tribes of birds sang.

—Walther von der Vogelweide, *Dream Song*

CONTENTS

Introduction

Creating a Paradise for Birds 8

Chapter 1

Planning a Bird-Friendly Garden . .12

Chapter 2

Plants for Attracting Birds 40

Chapter 3

Elements for Luring Birds 66

Chapter 4

Enjoying the Birds 92

Plant Hardiness Zones 120

Sources 121

Further Reading 123

Index 125

INTRODUCTION

CREATING
A PARADISE
FOR BIRDS

Left: A garden filled with a variety of
fruiting, flowering, and foliage plants
will provide the food and cover
that backyard birds crave.
Above: A male painted bunting
greatly enjoys his bath.

Below: **An apple serviceberry (*Amelanchier* x *grandiflora*) serves as a centerpiece in this bird-friendly border. The small tree provides both cover and edible fruits for birds, while the selection of pink and scarlet monardas (*Monarda* spp.) planted beneath it are a sure lure for hummingbirds. The tube feeder is an extra draw for songbirds.**

Birds make wonderful companions, twittering and singing, hopping and swooping through the garden. They aid the garden, and thus the gardener, by dispersing seed and pollinating plants and by eating bugs and grubs. These beautiful, breathing garden ornaments bring life to the garden, both literally and metaphorically, adding the important dimension of movement to a world filled with firmly rooted plants. It's a joy to watch them flit from tree to tree, gathering material for their nests or food for their fledglings.

Many of us feel lucky when we look up to see a winged visitor hopping across the lawn or serenading us from a nearby branch, but attracting birds to your garden needn't be a matter of happenstance. There are simple, specific things that you can do to make your backyard a haven for birds, even as you create a beautiful outdoor space for your family and friends to enjoy, and this book tells you exactly how.

While viewing birds is certainly pleasurable, there's an even greater reason to create a safe environment for birds. An important part of the ecosytem,

Left: **With just a bit of effort, any backyard can become a haven for birds. In addition to the tall trees, which offer shelter, the birds who visit here find a variety of feeders and a ready source of fresh water.**

birds are under increasing threat due to shrinking habitats, disturbed migration routes, deadly pesticides, and other side effects of expanding human civilization. Making your garden a welcoming spot for birds helps assure the continued presence of these wild creatures, strengthening the entire web of life in your neighborhood ecosystem. Families concerned about the environment and interested in doing their part will find bird fostering a fun and rewarding activity that has the added benefit of teaching young children a sense of stewardship of the earth.

This book gives you all the practical information you need to turn your own backyard into a bird-friendly zone, with plenty of hints and tips for attracting many different birds. Chapter 1, Planning a Bird-Friendly Garden, shows you how to entice birds to set up residence by arranging your landscape to meet these creatures' simple needs. Chapter 2 guides you in selecting the plants that birds adore, focusing as well on the particular flowers and trees that draw the kind of birds you'd most like to have as guests.

Elements for Luring Birds, Chapter 3, shares the secrets of choosing supplemental features—such as nest boxes, birdbaths, and bird feeders—that really work. Chapter 4, Enjoying the Birds, offers tips and ideas for making the most of your new bird paradise, with a regional guide to the birds you are most likely to see in your own backyard.

With lots of useful plant lists and charts that help you understand bird behavior, as well as recipes and tip boxes, this beautifully illustrated book is the perfect companion for the bird-loving gardener.

CHAPTER 1

PLANNING A BIRD-FRIENDLY GARDEN

Left: **Gardens with a wild touch are among the most successful at attracting birds.**

Above: **A brilliantly colored male cardinal snacks on a seed.**

All too often, homeowners hang up a pretty painted birdhouse, sit back, and wait for the bird family to move in. And all too often, spring turns to summer and autumn turns to winter with no more than the usual number of bird visitors to the garden, none of which show the slightest interest in the Victorian cottage in the sky. It takes more than a birdhouse to lure these winged crea-

tures. (Actually, many birdhouses are unattractive, if not downright harmful, to birds.)

But birds' needs are not difficult to meet. In fact, they require the same basic necessities that humans need to thrive: food, water, and shelter. But these three elements must not only be accessible, they must be arranged in a way that makes the birds feel safe and secure.

SURVEY YOUR GARDEN

Before buying your first sunflower seed, take a good look at your yard to assess its bird-friendliness. Sometimes the very areas you consider problems are the foundation of a bird haven. Perhaps there's a dead tree in that little grove at the back of your lot, or maybe there's a stand of tall, fence-hugging grasses that you've been meaning to mow down. Before you clean up your yard, remember that an overly manicured landscape is not a good place for birds to live and raise families.

Below: **Before you make changes, review elements you already have. Tall trees or wooded areas, dense plantings, and native flowers such as this red bee balm (*Monarda didyma*) and pink phlox (*Phlox* spp.) are all ingredients for a successful bird garden.**

Below: **This Arizona garden features plants native to the West, such as *Penstemon parryii*. Planning a garden in keeping with the character of your regional landscape makes it easier to match plants to cultural conditions.**

Often, gardening for the birds is a matter of unlearning some of our long-honored gardening traditions. Heavily pruned trees, tightly sheared shrubs, carpets of short-cut grass, isolated island beds of exotic annuals, and stiff, hybridized tea roses regularly misted with chemical pesticides combine to make a bird's worst nightmare. Birds have always embraced the idea of the natural garden, and modern homeowners are now catching up. Let nature be your guide when you are planning a bird-friendly garden—remember that Mother Nature has protected her bird species for millennia. Shady woodlands, wildflower-dotted meadows, dry deserts punctuated by prickly cactus, and boggy stands of cattails all harbor happy birds. Choosing a garden style that suits your region and your garden space is much easier than working against nature. A mix of plants in varied forms, textures, and sizes is the most effective

way to be sure birds are secure (see Chapter 2 for suggestions on specific plants).

But it's not enough to plant a bird-attracting shrub and expect that birds will begin to frequent your yard. A bird out in the open is a bird vulnerable to predators. To feel comfortable, birds need a variety of places where they can perch safely and they need secure avenues of cover that they can use to move about the yard. Planting plenty of trees, shrubs, tall grasses, and wildflowers at different heights and in natural-looking drifts, and using these plants to help integrate features such as feeders and birdbaths, gives the birds places to hide in the event that a hawk or a cat happens along.

When you survey your yard, take a pad of paper with you and jot down all the features you have that you want to keep. Then, as you read through this book and do further research on the elements you'd like to add, make a separate column for your wish list. Many gardeners find it helpful to also draw a garden plan on a piece of graph paper. This way, you will be able to plan with the garden's scale in mind, and can allow for the eventual size of plants, the appropriate distances of nest boxes, and so on. Don't panic if the work and expense of creating your ideal bird-lover's garden seems overwhelming at first. Almost all gardens are works in progress, and your bird-lover's garden will likely be no different. You can add a plant or an element here and there, as you have time and money. The birds will appreciate even a modest effort, and with a plan in hand, you will be working efficiently toward your ultimate goal.

HEDGEROWS

While we in North America consider a hedge to be a sort of living fence—a neatly clipped, dense, growing barrier—the hedgerows of the old country, especially those in England and Ireland, are wilder and more varied. (Originally, hedges were made out of dried brush, wooden pickets, or stone, and delineated boundaries of estates or political districts; they also served to corral livestock and to contain fields of crops.)

These old-fashioned hedgerows extended over vast tracts of land, and harbored a multitude of birds, who felt protected by the densely growing bushes. Many of the traditional hedging plants even provide food for birds. Consider planting an old-style hedgerow to define your garden space. Not only will you be attracting lots of birds, you'll also be adding an attractive feature in its own right, one that blocks unwanted sounds and screens visual "noise," as well as ornamenting your garden space. Following you'll find suggestions for good hedge plants.

EVERGREEN HEDGES

Abelia grandiflora (glossy abelia)

Bambusa multiplex riviereorum (Chinese godess bamboo)

Bambusa spp. (bamboo)

Berberis buxifolia (Magellan barberry)

Berberis darwinii (Darwin barberry)

Buxus microphylla japonica (Japanese boxwood)

Buxus sempervirens (English boxwood)

Camellia japonica (Japanese camellia)

Carpinus betulus 'Fastigiata' (European hornbeam)

Chamaecyparis lawsoniana (Port Orford cedar)

Cocculus laurifolius (laurel-leaf cocculus)

Cupressocyparis leylandii (Leyland cypress)

Elaeagnus pungens (silverberry)

Escallonia rubra (ruby escallonia)

Euonymus fortunei (evergreen euonymus, wintercreeper)

Ilex spp. (holly)

Juniperus spp. (juniper)

Ligustrum japonicum (Japanese privet)

Ligustrum spp. (privet)

Mahonia aquifolium (Oregon grape)

Myrtus communis (true myrtle)

Nandina domestica (heavenly bamboo)

Osmanthus heterophyllus (false holly)

Photinia fraseri (Fraser photinia)

Pinus strobus (eastern white pine)

Podocarpus macrophyllus (yew pine)

Prunus laurocerasus (English laurel cherry)

Prunus lustanica (Portugal laurel)

Pyracantha spp. (firethorn)

Rhaphiolepis indica (India hawthorn)

Rhododendron spp. (rhododendron)*

Taxus spp. (yew)

Thuja spp. (American arborvitae)

Viburnum spp. (viburnum)*

Xylosma congestum 'Compacta' (compact xylosma)

*May be deciduous, depending on location or cultivar

DECIDUOUS HEDGES

Acer campestre (hedge maple)

Berberis mentorensis
  (mentor barberry)

Berberis thunbergii
  (Japanese barberry)

Cornus mas (cornelian cherry)

Corylus avellana (filbert, hazel)

Cotoneaster acutifolius
  (Peking, hedge cotoneaster)

Crataegus spp. (hawthorn)

Euonymus alata
  (winged burning bush)

Fagus sylvatica (European beech)

Forsythia intermedia
  (forsythia, goldenbell)

Ligustrum 'Vicaryi'
  (vicary golden privet)

Lonicera korolkowii 'Zabeli'
  (Zabel's honeysuckle)

Malus spp. (crabapple)

Sophora japonica
  (Japanese pagoda tree)

Syringa spp. (lilac)

Xylosma congestum (shiny xylosma)

Juniperus virginiana
'Gray Owl'

BECOME AN ORGANIC GARDENER

Below: **During spring and early summer, the diet of the melodious mockingbird consists mainly of insects. Because insecticides endanger birds that eat poisoned insects, organic gardening is a critical part of gardening for birds.**

Organic gardening practices are essential to maintaining a healthy environment for birds. If you are using pesticides in your garden, you are poisoning insects, which are in turn poisoning your birds. Among the birds that eat insects are bluebirds, bushtits, chimney swifts, mockingbirds, Northern orioles, phoebes, swallows, warbling vireos, winter wrens, and yellow warblers. If the chemical pesticides succeed in eliminating the insects, you are also eliminating a food source for these birds. Instead of pesticides, consider companion plantings or biological controls such as importing ladybugs into the garden. If you are attracting lots of birds to your garden, they will keep most insect populations in check without the use of harmful chemicals.

In fact, as a gardener for the birds, it will be your business to attract insects to your garden. You will not, of course, want to draw bugs that will decimate your plants, but you will want to make a home for a wide variety of bees, butterflies, beetles, and other insects. Consider planting good nectar producers such as grape hyacinth, butterfly bush, valerian, bee balm, yarrow, and goldenrod. There are bound to

GROW YOUR OWN INSECT REPELLENT

Keep insects away from your most valuable plants with a home-grown insect spray. Grow chamomile, chives, mint, oregano, sage, and/or yarrow. Harvest the leaves and flowers of at least two (though you can add more) of these plants and boil them in a large pot full of water until you have a strong brew. Add hot pepper to the mix, and let the solution cool thoroughly before spraying on plants.

be a wealth of other excellent bee-magnet plants in your region, so ask a local nurseryman or an avid neighborhood gardener what they'd recommend.

In addition to pesticides, some gardeners use chemical fertilizers and disease controls to nourish and protect their plants. This may seem to work beautifully in the short run, but in the long run may be not only harmful to birds but also to the health of the garden. The best way to nurture your plants is with rich, well-conditioned garden soil, and the best way to get rich, well-conditioned soil is by adding compost. It's not difficult to make your own heap, in which you can "manufacture" compost, but if you don't have the time to wait or the space to devote to it, you can also buy compost at any garden center or even at most large discount chains. Dig compost in when preparing the soil, and add it as top-dressing, too.

TRY THE SOAP SOLUTION

If the bugs are truly running rampant in your garden, try an insecticidal soap, available at garden centers, rather than spraying a chemical pesticide. You can also mix your own: stir 2 teaspoons of dishwashing liquid (don't use the kind intended for dishwashers) into a gallon of water and spray affected plants. Wet the plants thoroughly with the solution, and repeat this treatment every few days for two weeks.

For the best start to your garden, get a soil test done. This is usually easily accomplished by purchasing a soil test kit at a garden center. You simply add some of your garden soil to an envelope and send it off to a soil laboratory, which then returns an

Below: **About a third of this female cardinal's diet consist of insects, including common garden pests such as aphids, grasshoppers, scale insects, snails, and slugs. She also feeds on fruits and seeds.**

21

Opposite: **Choosing plants that will be happy in their situation and arranging them in natural-looking drifts around water features and other bird-attracting elements creates a garden that approximates the wild environment where birds thrive.**

Below: **Features for birds can be both practical and decorative. A birdhouse painted on the outside won't harm the birds and can accent your plantings beautifully.**

EASY COMPOSTING

Composting methods are hotly debated among experienced gardeners, and the proportions, timing, turning, container, temperature, and so on are all factors that need a fair amount of attention if you are in a hurry for your compost. The easy method is quite a bit slower. Simply create a small heap in an out-of-the-way spot and add kitchen and garden scraps as you produce them. Never add any meat or bones (they'll attract rats and other undesirables) and don't add weeds that have gone to seed or diseased plant parts, or you'll be spreading mayhem throughout your garden when you use the compost.

All you have to do is loosen the pile from time to time using a pitchfork or a shovel; complete turning isn't necessary. Make sure to structure your pile in the shape of a mountain, so that water runs off the top. If your climate is very rainy, you'll need to cover the pile with a piece of plastic or a tarp; moisture is good, but a pile that is constantly waterlogged is not.

The best time to start your compost pile is in the autumn, when plenty of fallen leaves are available to create a good base. If you live in a climate where the weather is temperate in the winter, you will most likely have usable compost by springtime. If your winter weather is freezing, the compost will go dormant in the cold, and will start to heat up and decompose again in the spring. You can then add to the pile all summer long, and will probably have good compost by autumn.

analysis of your soil with specific suggestions on how to correct any deficiencies. Take the suggestions to heart: good soil will give your plants their best chance for success.

Taking a few simple precautions can prevent disease from wreaking havoc in your garden. First, whenever possible, choose plants that are disease-resistant and well-adapted to their situations. A thirsty plant that is stressed by drought or a sandy-soil-loving herb growing in clay is more susceptible to diseases. Also be sure to plant seeds and transplants at proper distances; overcrowding retards air circulation, which can lead to fungal diseases. Water plants at the base to avoid wetting leaves, which can create conditions favorable for funguses.

Be vigilant in spotting the early signs of disease. As you stroll through your garden, check your plants: leaves with white deposits are an indication of mildew, while brown, red, or orange spots on the undersides of leaves generally mean they've got a case of rust. Blackspot is, not surprisingly, indicated by black spots on plant leaves. If you are well-acquainted with the plants in your garden, you are likely to notice when one of them is looking peaked. Pick off the affected leaves immediately and dispose of them in tightly tied plastic garbage bags or by burning them in a trash can (some local ordinances prohibit this, so be sure to check with authorities before burning any type of trash). In more severe cases, you may need to prune out larger portions of the affected plant.

23

COMPANION PLANTING

Concerned gardeners are always looking for ways to avoid insecticides and other garden chemicals, and in recent years the idea of companion planting—which was used by gardeners long before chemical pesticides were even concocted—has enjoyed an inspired renaissance. A time-honored tradition, companion planting works on the theory that certain plants, by virtue of their aroma or unsavory plant juices, deter some insects and diseases. While investigators have found scientific bases for the effectiveness of some plant combinations, no one is sure why others seem to work. Some gardeners declare that the recommended combinations don't work in their gardens, while others swear by them. If you want to minimize pests in an organic way, companion planting is certainly worth a try. You'll notice that qualifying as an insect-repellent generally involves a strong odor. Below are some of the top choices.

Right: **Chives**

(*Allium schoenoprasum*)

Basil

Calendula

Chives

Coriander

Garlic

Geraniums

Marigolds (scented types)

Mints

Nasturtiums

Onions

Pennyroyal

Radishes

Rosemary

Sage

Tansy

Thyme

Wormwood

Following are some of the most common companion plant pairings, with the protected plant(s), its "guard" plant(s), and the pest it's said to repel. Note that many of the plants targeted for protection are vegetables; it's not surprising that the prevailing lore concerns them, since these food crops have long been among the most valued garden denizens. If you have a kitchen plot in your yard, try some of these suggestions to prevent unwanted insect visitors.

PLANT TO PROTECT	GUARD PLANT	PEST REPELLED
Apple trees	Nasturtiums	Aphids
Asparagus	Basil, calendula, parsley, tomatoes	Asparagus beetles
Broccoli, Cabbage, Cauliflower	Hyssop, mint, rosemary, sage, thyme, wormwood	Cabbage butterfly
	Thyme, tomatoes	Cabbage maggots, flea beetles
Carrots	Onions	Rust flies
	Rosemary	Carrot flies
	Parsley	Carrot beetles
Corn	Geraniums, scented marigolds	Various corn pests
Cucumbers	Radishes, nasturtiums	Cucumber beetles
Eggplant	Catnip	Flea beetles
Green beans	Potatoes, scented marigolds, summer savory	Mexican bean beetles
	Onions	Ants
Peach trees	Onions, garlic	Borers
	Nasturtiums	Aphids
Potatoes	Green beans, horseradish	Colorado potato beetles
Plum trees	Horseradish	Ants
Raspberries	Garlic	Beetles
Roses	Scented marigolds	Nematodes
	Chives	Aphids
	Garlic	Ants
	Tansy	Japanese beetles
Squash	Nasturtiums, radishes	Squash bugs
Tomatoes	Basil, borage	Tomato hornworms
	Calendulas, scented marigolds	Many insects
	Tansy, wormwood	Flea beetles

Right: **This landscape draws on both the artistry of nature and the guidance of the gardener. Rocks in different sizes and shapes create a natural-looking waterfall, and ferns and mosses soften the craggy surfaces. Narcissus drift casually through the scene.**

LET IT BE

Resist the urge to tidy your garden up too much. Some cleanup is, of course, essential to the health of the garden, but you'll want to leave plenty of areas where birds can shelter, as well as spots where they can search for insects. Using leaf litter as mulch encourages birds to scratch through it searching for bugs. Leaving the dried seedheads of flowers and grasses alone provides birds with a source of food through autumn and winter.

You will be most successful in attracting birds to your garden if you try to replicate, on a smaller scale, the elements of a wild landscape. The trick is to find the proper balance of features, so that your garden is a beautiful and well-kept part of the neighborhood as well as a retreat for the birds. Neither you nor your neighbors are likely to be all that happy with a yard that looks overgrown or weedy. The solution is often to alternate wild areas with those that are more traditionally tended. A meadow or prairie garden segmented by a wide mown path and bordered by a rustic fence looks intentional rather than unkempt. A small stream banked with plants takes on a new dimension when a small bridge or a series of stepping stones spans its width. Open areas of lawn punctuated with wide, informal beds and borders can offer shelter, food, and passageways for the birds, but give the impression of a more traditional garden.

The possibilities for integrating wild elements into your cultivated garden are almost endless, and all it takes is a bit of creativity. For inspiration, you might make a visit to some of your favorite ponds, forests, and meadowlands. Take note of the plants growing nearby and of the way nature arranges herself, and borrow some ideas for your garden (but never, never "borrow" plants from the wild). Notice the birds that congregate in these places, and see what you can do to duplicate their favorite haunts in your own yard.

Left: **Even a traditional garden can incorporate bird-friendly elements. This rose garden is bordered by an unmortared stone wall planted with shrubs and hostas and accented by a bird table. The wall and stone path lend a sense of structure while the plants provide food and cover for birds.**

27

Right: **Planting flowers, shrubs, and trees that are native to your region makes life easier for both you and the birds—you get a lovely, low-maintenance garden and the birds get tried-and-true food and cover sources. A planting of bee balm (*Monarda didyma*), purple coneflowers (*Echinacea purpurea*), and blazing stars (*Liatris* spp.) approximates a meadow or woodland edge, where insects and the birds that eat them will flock.**

GO NATIVE

Planting species native to your region is a sure way to attract birds. Birds have evolved over millennia to expect certain plants in certain areas, and they have long-developed tastes for the seeds, fruits, and nectars native to the region where they are living. This is not to say that they don't appreciate other types of plants and supplemental feeding, particularly in harsh weather, but generally birds' diets have been well established by native availability over many, many thousands of years. (See Chapter 2 for more about planting for the birds.)

A benefit of landscaping with native plants is that they are generally easy to grow because they are adapted for the conditions in your region. They'll need less attention from you, so you'll have more time to enjoy your birds and your garden.

Growing native plants also lends your garden a strong sense of regional character and helps to integrate your yard into the larger landscape. Visiting local parks and botanical gardens will give you an appreciation of the plants that grow well in your part of the country, while local garden clubs and horticultural societies are usually happy to offer advice.

Many native species have traits, such as rich fragrance or an abundance of nectar, that may have been hybridized out of modern cultivars. If you are planning on purchasing a cultivated variety of a plant (and in many cases you may want certain new cultivars for their ornamental value, increased hardiness, or resistance to pests or diseases), be sure to ask the nursery if the plant has retained its bird-attracting qualities.

GIVE A YEAR-ROUND BANQUET

Birds benefit from a healthy selection of their favorite foods growing in the garden, as well as from supplemental offerings at bird feeders, especially in the depth of winter. Fruiting trees and shrubs, together with grasses and flowers that bear snack-worthy seeds, are ideal choices for your bird haven. Planning for year-round provisions helps keep the birds happy, healthy, and flocking to your garden. (See Chapter 2 for the best plants for attracting birds.)

Left: **Backyard birds need plenty of food to raise healthy offspring. Filling your garden with fruit-bearing shrubs and grasses and flowers that provide seeds will encourage bird couples to take up residence in your yard.**

Different birds have different food preferences, and learning the favorite treats of the birds you want to attract will give you greater success in drawing them. (See Chapter 3 for more about the specific supplemental foods and feeder types that various birds favor.)

A garden design that includes a variety of fruiting plants that bear in succession throughout the year ensures a good turnout of birds. Spring and summer are easy times for birds, as nature is awash with insects and fresh fruits. Wild strawberries are excellent choices for groundcovers, and their fruit is adored by birds. Any fruit tree is sure to be a success—try cherry, apricot, or peach trees. Berry bushes, too, make perfect natural bird feeders, with raspberries, elderberries, and blueberries leading the pack in terms of bird favorites. Grapes will also be deeply appreciated.

Viburnums and sumacs take over the duties in autumn, and birds flock to their shining fruits. In winter, birds are drawn to the fruits of the holly, pyracantha, and cotoneaster. It is in the winter season that birds rely most on their human friends. Feeders filled with nutritious seeds and suet help keep the birds that have stuck around healthy 'til spring.

Hummingbirds, those buzzing, glittering gems of the bird world, have their own special needs, and feed primarily on insects and flower nectar. Hummers are attracted by bright flowers, particularly red and orange, and prefer blooms in tubular shapes, like those of the trumpet vine.

Don't Forget the H₂O

Like all living things, birds need water. A ready supply of fresh water will soon register with birds in your area, and they'll remember the source when they need it. Insect- and seed-eaters usually require more drinking water than birds that eat fruit, but whatever their diet, all birds will appreciate a good water source. Remember that water is especially important to birds in times of drought or in the winter, when available water is far less plentiful.

While birds can find often find water to drink from a variety of sources, such as puddles and dew on leaves, there isn't always enough to bathe in, so they'll be delighted to find a birdbath in your garden.

Insect-eaters generally won't visit a feeder, so supplying water will draw birds you may not otherwise have an opportunity to see. Especially in dry regions such as the desert Southwest, birds will be reliably attracted by the promise of ample fresh water.

Bathing keeps feathers in good condition, and is necessary to the health of a bird. By soaking, splashing, and shaking themselves, then preening, birds rid themselves of dirt and dust. Birds need their feathers to fly, but also to keep themselves warm in winter and cool in summer.

Integrate a birdbath or another small water feature into your garden, and you'll find a variety of visitors there daily. Do consider that birds are vulnerable when bathing: the neighborhood cat or a passing hawk can swoop in and catch a bird at the moment when it is thoroughly waterlogged and

Opposite: **Winter is a critical time for survival, and birds particularly appreciate trees and shrubs that provide fruit late in the season. This cedar waxwing revels in the abundant supply of hawthorn berries he's found.**

Below: **A supply of fresh water for drinking and bathing is a key ingredient in attracting birds to the garden.**

unable to fly very far. Placing your birdbath beneath a tree but several yards away from concealing shrubs will shield songbirds from the overhead gaze of a predatory bird and give them an emergency perch, but will prevent a cat from sneaking up unannounced. (For more on choosing a good birdbath and siting it properly, see Chapter 3.)

GIVE 'EM SHELTER

Setting up a feeder or growing some sunflowers will certainly attract birds to your garden, but the birds are not necessarily there to stay. They may very well show up for dinner, then eat and run. To get birds to set up residence, or at least to spend a significant part of their day in your garden, you'll need to meet their need for shelter as well as for water and food.

Tall trees and shrubs and vines growing in thickets make birds feel safe. If the bushes have sharp thorns or prickly stems, so much the better. A tangle of wild roses or a brambly patch of raspberries offer good protective cover and have the added bonus of attractive flowers and edible fruit. If you live in a desert climate, large cacti such as saguaro and prickly pear serve much the same function.

Evergreens, with their dense, prickly leaves or needles, are among the best shelters for birds. In addition to providing a refuge from predators, they provide a place where birds can perch protected from harsh weather. If evergreen trees or shrubs don't fit into your plan, consider planting vines along a wall, where birds can shelter.

SHELTERING EVERGREENS

Birds will make their homes in a variety of evergreen shrubs and trees. Do think about the eventual size of the evergreen, and make sure that you can accommodate it in your garden. You'll also want to be sure that the tree won't shade the house excessively when it is full grown. Because individual species vary widely in their eventual height, check catalog or nursery descriptions carefully before purchasing an evergreen, or indeed any tree or shrub.

Firs (*Abies* spp.)

Hollies (*Ilex* spp.)

Junipers (*Juniperus* spp.)

Spruces (*Picea* spp.)

Pines (*Pinus* spp.)

Hemlocks (*Tsuga* spp.)

Opposite: **Evergreens provide the best shelter for birds, but deciduous trees, shrubs, and vines will also serve. Here, a birdhouse in a copse of evergreens is extra enticement for cavity-nesters to set up residence.**

Below: **A dark-eyed junco sits on the snow-covered branch of an evergreen. In the depth of winter, the tree's dense, prickly needles provide much-needed shelter for resident birds.**

Above: Dense branches spiked with dangerous thorns conceal the cup-shaped nest of a song sparrow. The birds will be able to raise their nestlings in safety within the embrace of this blackberry bush.

Be aware that some species travel in flocks, especially in winter, and these birds will need ample space for all to settle down for the night. If you plant several sheltering trees together you're more likely to attract these types of birds.

While cover in the form of shrubs and trees is essential for birds, you'll also need to minimize roaming cats in your garden. Keep your family pets indoors (while dogs can't usually catch a healthy bird, they will chase them away) and report strays to your local ASPCA.

A Place to Call Home

When you think of nesting birds, you most often picture a pair of birds building a twiggy bowl-shaped structure in the crook of a shade tree. While there are certainly plenty of birds that behave in this way, including robins, jays, and wood thrushes, you'll be surprised by the variety of nesting sites and construction techniques that exist throughout the bird world.

Lots of birds prefer hollows in dead trees to nests in the branches of a live one. These are the cavity-nesters, and include woodpeckers, chickadees, nuthatches, titmouses, and house wrens. If you have a dead tree in your yard, or even a large, dead limb on a living tree, consider leaving it in place for its bird-attracting powers. Do be sure, first, that the tree will not hit a house, street, or sidewalk if it should topple over. Cavity-nesters will feel at home in birdhouses and nest boxes, too, as long as the house is the appropriate size and dimension for the species (see page 84 for more on birdhouses and nest boxes).

Many birds feel most secure nesting in dense thickets or patches of brambles. Catbirds, cardinals, mockingbirds, and the ever-popular goldfinches are just a few of these, and you can up your odds of attracting them by planting thorny shrubs and

Below: **Consider allowing dead or felled trees to remain in your garden. An upright dead tree attracts cavity-nesting birds, while fallen ones are rife with the insects birds treasure. This creative gardener has made a planter out of a new stump by hollowing out the top and filling it with greenery and mosses.**

entangling vines, such as raspberries or wild roses along with honeysuckle or morning glories. Plan for the shrubs to encompass an area of about 8 feet by 8 feet (2.4m by 2.4m) in order to allow enough room for nesting.

Still other birds, like meadowlarks and bobolinks, prefer open grassy spaces like unmown meadows.

Opposite: **Open grassy areas or flower-filled meadows punctuated or bordered by dense shrubbery and tall trees provide ideal habitats for many birds, including goldfinches, buntings, and sparrows. This sophisticated meadow planting makes use of garden favorites such as phlox (*Phlox* 'Franz Schubert), poppies (*Papaver* spp.), Eryngium, and chives (*Allium schoenoprasum*).**

CONSTRUCTION MATERIALS

Offering birds nesting materials is easy, low-cost, and fun. It's a great activity to do with kids, who can then try to discover where the birds are building their nests. Do be sure to warn chidren, however, not to approach a nest site. The birds will be disturbed and may abandon the site, and territorial birds may try to defend their nest or fledglings by swooping at kids' heads.

Following is a list of some favorite nesting materials. You can drape them from trees, pile them on old stumps, or put them in mesh bags and hang them from feeders. Never include sewing thread or fishing line in your nest offerings, as the birds may get tangled up in them. Also make sure that lengths of thicker twine or string do not exceed 4 inches (10cm), for the same reason.

Yarn

Twine

Bakery string

Old feathers

Goose or duck down

Rabbit or dog fur

Horsehair

Twigs

Evergreen needles

Dried grass

As you plot your garden and plan your bird-attracting features, it's easy to get overwhelmed by the sheer number of possibilities. Don't feel compelled to follow every directive or plant every bird-cherished flower and shrub. Birds are bound to appreciate even minimal gestures, and a few key elements may be all you need to turn your yard into a healthy environment for the birds.

When you plan and plant your bird-lover's garden, don't forget to make a space for yourself. This small summerhouse, tucked back in a corner of the garden, is a perfect spot for observing the garden's fluttering guests. Even a bench or a simple seat will offer a comfortable spot from which to appreciate your handiwork.

CHAPTER 2

PLANTS FOR ATTRACTING BIRDS

Above: A cedar waxwing with the berry of an Eastern red cedar.

Left: Sunflowers (*Helianthus* spp.) are champion bird-attractors.

Above: **This garden is a true haven for birds, with its sunny grass- and flower-filled clearing surrounded by hazel, birch, and hawthorn.**

Fortunately for gardeners, the plants that birds like are often those that we like, too. And many plants attractive to songbirds are also favorite nectar and host plants for butterflies and hummingbirds. So filling your garden with bird-friendly trees, shrubs, grasses, and flowers is certainly no chore. In fact, the greatest challenge may be in narrowing your list.

42

WHICH PLANTS SHALL I CHOOSE?

You've already helped to define your garden by electing to make it attractive to birds, and this decision will inform, in some part, the plants that you choose. But there are a host of other considerations that will make deciding which plants to include in your bird-lover's garden much easier. Ask yourself the following questions when making up your plant wish list.

Does the plant fit into my garden space?

Consider the eventual size of the trees, shrubs, or perennials you are planting. While a grand fir may appear small and completely manageable in the nursery container, it may ultimately grow as tall as 200 feet (61m). Pruning a plant heavily to keep it in bounds can amount to a lot of work, and may ruin the informal habit that is so attractive to birds. You are best off choosing plants that will stay within the

Below: **A hungry tufted titmouse eyes a cluster of snow-covered, vitamin-rich rosehips. Plant roses that produce the colorful hips (not all do), and don't deadhead the flowers if you want the bush to set hips—the plump fruits will ripen in autumn and last well into winter.**

space you have allotted. The entries in this section include information about plant height; make sure to check catalog descriptions and nursery tags carefully for the specific dimensions of any cultivar or unfamiliar species you plan to purchase.

Will the plant grow happily in the conditions I have and with the care I am willing to give it?

A sunflower asked to grow in a shady woodland garden is just never going to succeed. While there are some plants that can adapt to almost any cultural situation, most have specific conditions they need to thrive: some require full sun, others need sandy soil, and still others insist on regular feeding. While you can certainly change some of the conditions in your garden, for instance by amending your soil or changing the grade of the land, plants that demand conditions not present will require a fair amount of maintenance. Ask yourself how much time and effort you are willing to devote to maintaining your garden. In the end, your plants will fare best, and you will stay most sane, if you are not constantly at odds with the conditions in your garden.

Does the plant suit my garden's character and does it fit into the color and design scheme I've selected?

Having a vision of how you want your garden to look will help you narrow down the plants you can add. You just have to remain focused when confronted with a dazzling array of blooming beauties in the glossy pages of catalogs and the aisles of well-stocked garden centers. Deciding in the planning stages that you want an informal, cottage-style garden of mainly pastels means that you can eliminate all the plants that don't fit into that scheme—plants with hot colors, formal habits, or exotic forms can automatically be removed from consideration. Many gardeners, however, don't work within such a defined theme. If you are one of these, you'll do best by envisioning where you'll put the new plant and thinking about how it will fit with the plants and features you already have or are planning to add. If you can't see it clearly, or if your vision is less than inspiring, you can probably skip it.

Does the plant have a variety of gifts to offer?

Especially when space is limited, you'll want plants that possess a number of appealing qualities. Compare the plants you are considering, and opt for those with more than one asset. While flowers are often the most noticeable virtue, they may also be relatively short-lived, so look for plants that share some of the following qualities: ornamental foliage, textured bark, architectural form, and attractive berries, fruits, or seedpods.

Opposite: **All the coneflowers—these are *Echinacea purpurea* 'White Swan'—bloom over a long period of time, drawing birds to their seedheads. The daisylike blooms are also attractive to butterflies, who visit for the sweet nectar.**

Right: **A red-headed woodpecker pauses before resuming its quest for insects and fruit. To attract this spectacular bird, plant plenty of berry-producing shrubs.**

MAKING SENSE OF HARDINESS ZONES

Below: **Purple hummingbird sage (*Salvia leucantha*) gets rave reviews from hummingbirds, bees, and butterflies alike. This is an example of a plant with limited hardiness (Zones 7 to 10) that gardeners further north may wish to try; it grows quickly and will usually flower in its first season, so may be grown as an annual.**

W hile there are many factors that determine a plant's suitability for a particular region (such as summer temperatures and typical rainfall amounts), assessing a plant's cold-hardiness is one of the most widespread gauges. The United States Department of Agriculture (USDA) has developed a map based on average annual minimum temperatures, with the North American continent divided into eleven zones (the map is included for your reference on page 120).

Because there's nothing more depressing than seeing a favorite (and likely expensive) shrub or perennial killed off by winter's freezing grip, it's wise to choose plants that tolerate the cold in your region. It's still possible, of course, to lose plants in a particularly harsh winter, but in general, plants marked for specific zones will fare well there. Conversely, it is sometimes possible to protect delicate plants with mulch or cut evergreen boughs, or by surrounding them with dried leaves packed into a tomato cage.

The descriptions in this section include the hardiness zone range for each plant; note that annuals, which complete their life cycle in one season, are not subject to hardiness zones because they will not be coming back the following season regardless of the winter weather. Some plants grown as annuals in northern regions do, however, survive as perennials in warm climates.

Offering a selection of trees, shrubs, flowers, and grasses that bloom and set seed and fruit throughout the season is the surest way to attract a variety of birds to your garden. Remember to plant in natural-looking drifts and to mimic wild places in the arrangement of your plants. Think of the edge of a woods: trees interspersed with shrubs, ferns, and shade-loving wildflowers gradually blending into an open, sunny space filled with grasses and cheerful blooms.

In the following section, you'll find a wide selection of songbird-attracting flowers, grasses and grains, vines, shrubs, and trees. Plants adored by hummingbirds follow in a special section all their own. All the plants featured here are relatively easily to grow and suitable for a variety of garden spaces. There are, of course, many more possibilities. Be aware of the natural cycles and rhythms in your area, tap into the knowledge of experienced local gardeners, and experiment with plants native to your region—you may just find a terrific plant that hasn't been featured in any bird books, but that works great for you in your yard. Meanwhile, the following are tried-and-true bird attractors that will give you a great base for your bird-lover's garden.

FLOWERS FOR SONGBIRDS

ASTER NOVAE-ANGLIAE
New England aster

New England aster (*Aster novae-angliae*) is a spectacular perennial autumn wildflower with daisylike blooms in mostly purple, pink, and white, with golden centers. To attract birds, asters must be allowed to go to seed after flowering. New England asters do best in full sun, but will tolerate some partial shade, and grow 3 to 6 feet (1–1.8m). These hardy perennials are cold-tolerant from Zones 3 to 8.

BIDENS ARISTOSA
Tickseed sunflower

Tickseed sunflowers (*Bidens aristosa*) are annuals with small, golden, daisylike flowers that bloom late in the summer. They prefer sun, but will take some partial shade. This plant has the habit of self-sowing vigorously, so plant them where you don't mind if they spread. Or you may wish to mulch around the plants to deter dropped seeds from taking root. Tickseed sunflowers grow to about 4 feet (1.2m) and, as annuals, can be grown in all zones. This plant is a virtual magnet for butterflies as well as for small birds, as it supplies rich nectar and plentiful seeds.

Left: **Tickseed sunflower**
(*Bidens aristosa*)

47

Above: **Cosmos**

(*Cosmos bipinnatus*)

Right: **Purple coneflower**

(*Echinacea purpurea* 'Magnus')

COSMOS SPP.
Cosmos

Cosmos are pretty summer annuals that come in shades of pink and purple as well as white (*Cosmos bipinnatus*) or in orange and yellow (*C. sulphureus*). Reaching up to 4 feet (1.2m) in height, these flowers are favorites of butterflies and bear seeds that draw small songbirds. Cosmos need lots of sun but aren't too particular about their soil.

ECHINACEA PURPUREA
Purple coneflower

Purple coneflowers (*Echinacea purpurea*) are purple, daisylike wildflowers that grow to 2 or 3 feet (60–90cm). Give them full sun and somewhat dry soil, and they'll grow quite happily from high summer into the autumn. This flower is a particular favorite of the ever-popular goldfinch, so if you want to attract these little birds, plant plenty of coneflowers. Perennials with a habit of self-sowing, they're hardy from Zone 3.

HELIANTHUS SPP.
Sunflowers

Sunflowers (*Helianthus* spp.) are among birds' most adored food plants. Both annual and perennial varieties abound. Note that perennial types self-seed vigorously, but this may not be a problem for you if the birds get most of the seeds. The sunflower's large cheery face is one of the most welcome sights for birds. These flowers are notoriously easy to grow—just plant them in full sun (though some perennial species will also grow in shade). Height varies widely depending on the species and cultivar, but they can easily grow to 10 feet (3m). The annual kinds can be grown in any climate. The perennial ones grow in Zones 4 to 10, depending on the species.

RUDBECKIA SPP.
Coneflowers

There are many different species of coneflower, most of which are perennial, though there are also annual species. The sunny yellow flowers are notoriously easy to grow, and in fact are well-regarded denizens along highways and back roads all across North America. Coneflower seeds may be foraged by chickadees, cardinals, finches, and sparrows, among others. Coneflowers like full sun and well-drained soils. Depending upon the species, they may grow to 4 feet (1.2m) tall and range in hardiness from Zones 3 to 9.

TITHONIA ROTUNDIFOLIA
Tithonia

Tithonia (*Tithonia rotundifolia*) is a tall-growing (to 8 feet [2.4m]), bushy annual with orange, daisy-like flowers that appear in late summer. Tithonia is happiest in full sun and has no special soil requirements; it's appropriate for all zones. Butterflies and hummingbirds as well as seed-eating birds adore this hot-colored beauty.

YUCCA FILAMENTOSA
Adam's needle

Adam's needle is an exotic-looking perennial that grows from 5 to 15 feet (1.5–4.5m) tall. The plant features immense swordlike leaves and large snowy white flowers that are followed by seedpods edible to birds. The flowers themselves are also a source of food; the nectar is mined by both orioles and hummingbirds. This hardy yucca can be grown from Zones 3 to 10.

ZINNIA SPP.
Zinnias

Zinnias (*Zinnia* spp.) are old-fashioned flowers that have made a comeback in recent years. There are both annual and perennials types, and their bright, daisylike flowers are always a welcome sight for both birds and humans. Reaching 1 to 3 feet (30–90cm), the annuals can be grown in all zones; the perennial species are hardy from Zones 5 to 10. These flowers are easy to grow, too, requiring only full sun and regular soil. Zinnias are a notorious favorite of finches.

Above: **Tithonia**

(*Tithonia rotundifolia*)

Below: **Zinnia (*Zinnia* spp.)**

GRASSES AND GRAINS

ALOPECURUS SPP.
Foxtail grasses

Foxtail grasses (*Alopecurus* spp.) are annuals with long, fuzzy tops that resemble bushy tails. Foxtail grasses need full sun and soil that drains reasonably well, but are otherwise easy to grow. This grass grows between 2 and 3 feet (60–90cm) tall and can be planted in all zones. The birds love the seeds, but do be careful because any that they miss will seed themselves and the grass will spread aggressively.

ANDROPOGON SPP.
Bluestems

Bluestems (*Andropogon* spp.) provide winter seeds for small birds. These perennial grasses, named for their blue-green flower stems, may grow to 10 feet (3m) or more, depending on the species. This grass is hardy from Zones 4 to 10, depending upon the species you plant.

MILIUM SPP.
Millets

Millets (*Milium* spp.) are grown as annuals, and are beloved by birds. Growing 1 to 2 feet (30–60cm) tall, millets are appropriate for all zones. They need well-drained soil in a sunny spot, but are otherwise undemanding.

SORGHUM BICOLOR
Sorghum

Sorghum (*Sorghum bicolor*), an annual grass, is sometimes known as broom corn. It requires well-drained soil in a sunny space, grows 3 to 5 feet (1–1.5m) tall, and can be sown in all zones. Sorghum's clustered seedheads are much sought by birds, particularly blackbirds.

TREES, LOW-GROWING SHRUBS, AND VINES

ACER SPP.
Maples

Maple trees (*Acer* spp.) produce seeds in summertime that are a favorite of birds, including bobwhites, cardinals, and purple finches. There are more than one hundred and fifty species of maple, so there is bound to be one that fits into your garden. Some species are native to North America, while many others hail from Asia. Maples vary in height depending on the species, ranging in general from 6 to 75 feet

Below: **Sorghum (Sorghum bicolor)**

(1.8– 23m). Zones vary as well, ranging from 3 to 9, depending on the species.

AMELANCHIER SPP.
Serviceberries

Serviceberries (*Amelanchier* spp.) are sometimes known as Juneberries or shadberries, because the fruits ripen when the shad are running. These attractive shrubs (there are also a few tree species) bear pretty white flowers in spring and small round fruits in summer. Birds from robin to woodpecker to cardinal are attracted by the luscious fruits. Varying in height, most grow to less than 30 feet (9m), though some do grow taller. Serviceberries range in hardiness, depending on the species, from Zones 3 to 9.

CORNUS FLORIDA
Flowering dogwood

Flowering dogwood (*Cornus florida*) is an ornamental tree that blooms with showy flowers in springtime which are followed by brilliant red fruits that are much appreciated by birds. Flowering dogwood grows best in partial shade or full sun, in a slightly moist situation, and is hardy from Zones 5 to 8.

FRAGRARIA SPP.
Wild strawberries

Wild strawberries (*Fragraria* spp.) are spreading groundcovers that bear white flowers and small red fruits. Like most fruits, wild strawberries do best in a sunny spot. Many birds, including robins, thrashers, and grosbeaks, are attracted to the fruits. *Fragraria virginiana* is an easy-to-grow perennial species hardy from Zones 4 to 9.

ILEX SPP.
Hollies

Hollies (*Ilex* spp.) are among the most valuable bird-attracting shrubs you can plant, as they provide fruits in the lean winter months. Their evergreen, protective prickly leaves also provide excellent cover for birds. Hollies vary widely in height, depending upon the cultivar and species you choose; you'll find one for any size garden, as they range from 3 to 50 feet (1–16m) Depending on the species you plant, the holly grows in either sun or shade and is hardy from Zones 5 to 9. Do note that you'll need both a male and a female specimen in order to get berry production.

MALUS SPP.
Crabapples

Crabapples (*Malus* spp.—a genus that also includes apple trees) are deciduous trees or shrubs that are enjoyed by a variety of birds, from woodpeckers to robins to mockingbirds and more. Crabapples are covered with white or pink fragrant blossoms in

Above: **Oregon holly (*Ilex aquifolium* 'Handsworth New Silver')**

Below: **Crabapple (*Malus* spp.)**

Above: **Black mulberry**
(*Morus nigra*)

Below: **Staghorn sumac**
(*Rhus typhina*) in autumn

spring that are followed by smallish fruits. Because plants in this genus may be either trees or shrubs and vary widely in size, make sure to get an estimate of the ultimate size and habit of the apple or crabapple you are buying. Depending upon the species, crabapples are hardy from Zones 3 to 9.

MORUS SPP.
Mulberries

Mulberries (*Morus* spp.) are deciduous trees that have small white, black, or dark purple berries that are beloved by birds. Mulberries grow quite tall, to 100 feet (30.5m), so make sure you have room for the

species you have selected. These trees grow in sun or partial shade, and are hardy from Zones 4 to 9.

PRUNUS SPP.
Cherries

Cherry trees (*Prunus avium*, *P. cerastus*, *P. pensylvanica*, *P. virginiana*) have a double attraction for birds: in spring, birds are thrilled by the insects that swarm to the cherry's masses of flowers. The fruits, which appear in summer, also attract their share of birds. Some cherry species can reach 100 feet (30.5 m) in height, while others stay much smaller, so be sure to check the nursery tag carefully for the ultimate size of the specific tree you are purchasing. Sun requirements and hardiness zone depend upon the species you plant, but note that most of these trees are quite cold-hardy, ranging from Zones 2 to 6.

RHUS SPP.
Sumacs

Sumacs (*Rhus* spp.) are shrubs (sometimes grown as small trees) with beautiful autumn color and small berries. Birds adore the autumn fruits. This shrub will grow in sun or light shade in average soil, and grows anywhere from 5 to 20 feet (1.5–6m), depending on the species. Hardy from Zones 4 to 9, it can withstand some dry weather.

ROSA SPP.
Roses

There are more than one hundred species of roses (*Rosa* spp.) and an uncountable number of cultivars. For the purpose of luring birds, the wild, or species, roses are generally best. The showy flowers in pink, white, or red are followed by small fruits known as hips. Rose hips are desired by a large number of bird species, including cardinals, bluebirds, vireo, grosbeaks, and chickadees. Rose bushes and climbers vary in height from 2 to 20 feet (60 cm–6m), and range in hardiness from Zones 2 to 8, depending on the species. Nearly all need full sun.

RUBUS SPP.
Blackberries and raspberries

Blackberries and raspberries belong to a large genus (*Rubus*) of brambles, most of which bear fruits highly attractive to birds. White flowers appear in spring and are followed by the fruits in summer. Shrubs form dense thickets that are also favorite nesting sites, and so these plants do double duty. Blackberries and raspberries may grow 2 to 10 feet (60cm–3m) or more, and are hardy in Zones 3 to 7, depending on the species.

SAMBUCUS SPP.
Elderberries

Elderberries (*Sambucus* spp.) attract a multitude of birds, and there are many pretty species, including those with blue, purple, black, or red berries. Be certain that you have the space for an elderberry before you plant; they may reach 10 feet (3m) or taller, depending on the species. They'll grow in sun or light shade, and do best in moist, fertile soil. Elderberries are hardy from Zones 4 to 9.

TSUGA SPP.
Hemlocks

Hemlocks (*Tsuga* spp.) are needle-leaved evergreen trees that bear small cones. Birds relish the seeds

Left: **Elderberry**

(***Sambucus canadensis***)

hidden in the cones and take refuge within the thick needles. This tree grows to 100 feet (30.5m) in partial to full shade, performing best in cool climates. It needs moist, fertile soil, and thrives in Zones 4 to 9, depending on the species you plant.

VACCINIUM SPP.
Blueberries

Blueberries (*Vaccinium* spp.) are among birds' favorite foods. These shrubs are very versatile, as they feature attractive spring flowers, delicious fruit, and lovely autumn color. They are also easy to grow, but do have a few cultural requirements. They need soil that is moist, fertile, and on the acidic side. Blueberry shrubs can range widely in height from lowbush varieties that reach only 1 foot (30cm) to highbush varieties that can grow as tall as 15 feet (4.5m), so be sure to check the ultimate size of the type you are buying. Blueberries grow in either sun or light shade, and thrive in Zones 4 to 9.

VIBURNUM SPP.
Viburnums

Viburnums (*Viburnum* spp.) may be evergreen or deciduous, depending on the species. Fragrant spring flowers and plentiful berries make viburnum a valuable ornamental as well as a powerful attractor for birds. Depending on the species, viburnums grow between 4 and 10 feet (1.2–3m) tall. Most viburnums are easy to grow, and there are species for almost every situation from sun to deep shade; they thrive in Zones 4 to 9.

VITUS SPP.
Wild grapes

Deciduous vines, grape plants (*Vitus* spp.) produce small flowers followed by plump fruits. Grapes are much sought by literally one hundred different species of birds. Generally speaking, grapes like moist, well-drained soil in full sun or partial shade. They do need some support, so make sure to give them something to clamber up. Depending on the species, wild grapes are hardy from Zones 3 to 9.

Above: **Orange tea viburnum (*Viburnum setigerum* 'Aurantiacum')**

Right: **Cedar waxwings are chiefly fruit- and berry-eaters—try planting cherries, blackberries, elderberries, or viburnums to attract them.**

TASTY BERRIES

Let this calendar of berry harvests guide you in planting shrubs and trees that will attract birds in a multitude of months.

June	Huckleberry (*Gaylussacia* spp., *Vaccinium* spp.), mulberry (*Morus* spp.), raspberries (*Rubus* spp.), boysenberries (*Rubus ursinus* var. *loganobaccus*), blueberries (*Vaccinium* spp.)
July	Chokeberry (*Aronia* spp.), highbush blueberry (*Vaccinium corymbosum*), spicebush (*Lindera benzoin*), viburnum (*Viburnum* spp.)
August	Arrowwood (*Viburnum acerifolium*), elderberry (*Sambucus* spp.), sand cherry (*Prunus besseyi*), snowberry (*Symphoricarpos albus*)
September	Asiatic sweetleaf (*Symplocos paniculata*), bayberry (*Myrica pensylvanica*), barberry (*Berberis* spp.), bittersweet (*Celastrus* spp.), buckthorn (*Rhamnus* spp.), dogwood (*Cornus* spp.), elderberry (*Sambucus* spp.), firethorn (*Pyracantha* spp.), hackberry (*Celtis* spp.), highbush cranberry (*Viburnum trilobum*), inkberry (*Ilex glabra*), maple-leaf viburnum (*Viburnum acerifolium*), sour gum (*Nyssa sylvatica*), winterberry (*Ilex verticillata*)
October through January	Bayberry (*Myrica pensylvanica*), highbush cranberry (*Viburnum trilobum*), inkberry (*Ilex glabra*), Japanese barberry (*Berberis thunbergii*), nannyberry (*Viburnum prunifolium*), Coralberry (*Symphoricarpos or biculatus.*), winterberry (*Ilex verticillata*)
January	Hawthorn (*Crataegus* spp.), holly (*Ilex* spp.), mountain ash (*Sorbus* spp.), firethorn (*Pyracantha* spp.)

Right: **A rose-breasted grosbeak rests in a chokeberry bush. Come summer, the showy flowers will give way to abundant, glossy red berries.**

Below: **Birches (*Betula* spp.)** are valued by gardeners for their graceful form and ornamental bark, but they are also appreciated by a wide variety of birds, who feast on the seeds, catkins, and flower buds.

BIRDS LOVE PLANTS

Songbirds, in general, love tall, sheltering trees, seed-bearing flowers, and fruiting shrubs, but there are some plants that certain birds particularly adore. Use the following guide to understand which birds you are most likely to see near which plants and to learn which plants to focus on for the birds you most want to draw. The birds listed are not the only birds you will see near those plants.

Trees	Birds Attracted
Alder (*Alnus* spp.)	Bobwhite, goldfinch, grouse, mourning dove, pheasant
American elm (*Ulmus americana*)	Black-capped chickadee, goldfinch, pine siskin
Birch (*Betula* spp.)	Blue jay, cedar waxwing, finch, junco, titmouse
Flowering crabapple (*Malus* spp.)	Finch, grosbeak, mockingbird, towhee
Flowering dogwood (*Cornus florida*)	Cedar waxwing, cardinal, vireo, woodpecker
Hawthorn (*Crataegus* spp.)	Bobwhite, grouse, purple finch, thrush
Linden (*Tilia* spp.)	Bobwhite, grouse, redpoll
Maple (*Acer* spp.)	Nuthatch, robin, pine siskin, song sparrow
Mountain ash (*Sorbus* spp.)	Bobwhite, catbird, oriole, robin, waxwing, woodpecker
Mulberry (*Morus* spp.)	Cardinal, cuckoo, goldfinch, mockingbird, robin, thrush
Norway spruce (*Picea abies*)	Cedar waxwing, finch, grosbeak, grouse, sapsucker
Red cedar (*Juniperus virginiana*)	All birds native to eastern US
Sour gum (*Nyssa sylvatica*)	Blue jay, robin, thrush, waxwing, woodpecker
White pine (*Pinus strobus*)	Bobwhite, nuthatch, pine siskin, warbler, woodpecker
White spruce (*Picea glauca*)	Chickadee, crossbill, finch, goldfinch, woodpecker

Vines	Birds Attracted
Bittersweet (*Celastrus* spp.)	Song and game birds
Hall's honeysuckle (*Lonicera japonica* 'Halliana')	Grouse, flicker, meadow lark, song sparrow
Matrimony vine (*Lycium* spp.)	Songbirds
Woodbine (*Parthenocissus* spp.)	Black-capped chickadee, flicker, eastern bluebird, mockingbird, robin, thrush, tufted titmouse, woodpecker

Shrubs	Birds Attracted
Arrowwood (*Viburnum acerifolium*)	Bluebird, catbird, flicker
Bayberry (*Myrica pensylvanica*)	Almost 100 bird species
Blackhaw (*Viburnum lentago*)	Thrush, waxwing, woodpecker
Black huckleberry (*Gaylussacia baccata*)	Bluebird, catbird, chickadee, grosbeak, robin, towhee
Buckthorn (*Rhamnus* spp.)	Finch, grouse, pheasant, thrasher, waxwing
Dogwood (*Cornus* spp.)	All birds
Elderberry (*Sambucus* spp.)	More than 100 bird species
Highbush blueberry (*Vaccinium corymbosum*)	More than 100 bird species
Honeysuckle (*Lonicera* spp.)	Just about all songbirds and hummingbirds
Inkberry (*Ilex glabra*)	Bluebird, bobwhite, catbird, chickadee, robin, titmouse
Rose (*Rosa* spp.)	Cedar waxwing, cardinal, robin, bluebird, mockingbird, grouse, goldfinch, vireo, chickadee, indigo bunting
Viburnum (*Viburnum* spp.)	Bluebird, bobwhite, flicker, robin, thrush, waxwing
Winterberry (*Ilex verticillata*)	Song and game birds

Flowers	Birds Attracted
Asters (*Aster* spp.)	Cardinal, chickadee, goldfinch, grouse, indigo bunting, sparrow, titmouse, towhee, turkey
Coneflowers (*Rudbeckia, Echinacea* spp.)	Cardinal, chickadee, goldfinch, house finch, nuthatch, purple finch, sparrow, titmouse
Sunflowers (*Helianthus* spp.)	Chickadee, goldfinch, house finch, meadowlark, mourning dove, quail, red-winged blackbird, tree sparrow, tufted titmouse

Above: **An American goldfinch female eats the seeds of a purple coneflower** (*Echinacea purpurea*).

Above: **Hummingbirds, like this glittering Anna's hummingbird, adore bright red flowers with tubular shapes.**

PLANTS FOR HUMMINGBIRDS

Hummingbirds have their own special needs when it comes to plants. They find particularly irresistible red or orange trumpet-shaped flowers filled with sweet nectar.

In the following pages you'll find a selection of plants that are proven hummingbird attractors, designed to give you a good start in providing natural food for these jewel-like little birds.

AGASTACHE SPP.
Hyssops

Hyssops (*Agastache* spp.) are a popular perennial for the herb garden, and are a favorite of hummingbirds. They have tiny flowers that grow on spikes. Sun-lovers, hyssops are hardy from Zones 4 to 10.

AQUILEGIA SPP.
Columbines

Pretty, unusual wildflowers, columbines (*Aquilegia* spp.) have long-spurred flowers that are a favorite of hummingbirds. This perennial is hardy from Zones 3 to 10.

BUDDLEIA DAVIDII
Butterfly bush

Butterfly bush (*Buddleia davidii*), true to its name, will draw swarms of butterflies to your garden, but it will also attract hummingbirds. The purple, conical flowers appear in summer. This shrub is hardy from Zones 5 to 9.

CAMPSIS RADICANS
Trumpetvine

Trumpetvine (*Campsis radicans*) is a quick-growing vine with brilliant orange tubular blossoms that combine the hummers' favorite shape with one of their choice colors. The only difficulty trumpetvine poses is that it may spread too aggressively for your tastes. It is hardy in Zones 5 to 9.

CHAENOMELES SPECIOSA
Flowering quince

Flowering quince (*Chaenomeles speciosa*) is a shrub that bears early spring flowers in red, pink, or coral. It is hardy from Zones 5 to 10.

CLEOME HASSLERANA
Cleome

Cleome (*Cleome hasslerana*) is an old-fashioned annual (all zones) with strange-looking pink, purple, or white flowers that explain their alternate common name, "spider flower."

DELPHINIUM SPP.
Delphiniums

Delphiniums (*Delphinium* spp.) are perennials that grow in large spikes and appear in white, blue, and purple. Many species are rather fragile, and may fade in hot summers. They are hardy in Zones 3 to 10, and are best planted in full sun.

FUCHSIA SPP.
Fuchsias

Fuchsias (*Fuchsia* spp.) have elegant bicolored flowers in pink and purple, red and white, and other beautiful combinations. Their drop-like flowers make them a popular choice for hanging baskets. In warmer climates (Zones 8 to 10), fuchsias are used as garden shrubs too, though they grow as annuals further north.

Above: **Fuchsia (*Fuchsia* spp.)**

Left: **Butterfly bush (*Buddleia davidii*)**

59

HEUCHERA SPP.
Coral bells

Coral bells (*Heuchera sanguinea* and *H.* × *brizoides*) are grown mainly for their attractive scalloped leaves, but they also bear small red, pink, or white flowers carried on long thin stems that rise above the foliage. The red varieties are most effective in attracting hummingbirds. Coral bells, perennial plants, are hardy from Zones 3 to 10 and are best planted in full sun.

Below: **Coral bells (*Heuchera sanguinea*)**

IMPATIENS WALLERANA
Impatiens, busy lizzies

Impatiens (*Impatiens wallerana*) is the most popular bedding plant in North America, well-loved for its summer-long bright red, white, orange, and lilac flowers. Perennial in Zones 9 and 10, this classic flower is grown as an annual throughout the rest of the continent.

MIRABILIS JALAPA
Four o'clock

Four o'clocks (*Mirabilis jalapa*) have flowers that are tubular in shape and come in red, yellow, pink, white, and some bicolors. They get their name from the fact that they bloom in late afternoon. While four o'clocks may be grown as perennials in hot climates (Zones 9 and 10), they are grown as annuals elsewhere.

MONARDA DIDYMA
Bee balm

Bee balm (*Monarda didyma*) is a perennial with oddly shaped flowers in scarlet, white, pink, or reddish purple. Its common name expresses the reason that this flower is popular with hummers—the nectar that draws the bees also attracts the dazzling little birds. It thrives in Zones 4 to 9, and performs best in full sun.

NEPETA SPP.
Catmints

Catmints (*Nepeta* spp.), perennial herbs, grow in low mounds and have attractive silver leaves and tiny bluish purple flowers. They are hardy from Zones 3 to 10.

NICOTIANA SPP.
Flowering tobacco

Flowering tobaccos (*Nicotiana* spp.) have the tubular blooms hummingbirds love, and they come in a wide variety of colors including pink, purple, white, and even lime green. Most species are annuals, though there is a perennial species hardy in Zones 9 and 10.

PELARGONIUM SPP.
Scented geraniums

Scented geraniums (*Pelargonium* spp.) are usually grown for their highly fragrant foliage, which comes in scents ranging from apple to chocolate to lemon.

While the small flowers are somewhat subtle, they nevertheless attract lots of hummingbirds. Scented geraniums are perennials in Zones 9 and 10, but are well-grown as annuals in more northerly regions.

PELARGONIUM × HORTORUM
Geranium

Geraniums (*Pelargonium × hortorum*) are showy flowers with red, pink, coral, or white blooms. Perhaps most often grown in containers, these easy-going plants are perennials in Zones 9 and 10, but are grown as annuals throughout the rest of the continent.

Below: **Lush edges of catmint (***Nepeta* x *faasenii***) are a hummingbird's delight. This free-blooming herb produces fragrant purple flowers that keep the little birds coming back time after time.**

PENSTEMON SPP.
Penstemons

Penstemons (*Penstemon* spp.) have tubular flowers that hummingbirds adore, but there is a catch—many penstemons are hard to grow. If you want to give these perennials a try, make sure that your soil is well-drained and plant them in full sun. They are hardy from Zones 3 to 9, depending on the species.

PETUNIA SPP.
Petunias

A favorite annual all across North America, petunias (*Petunia* spp.) are widely used in both garden plots and containers. The showy blooms, which come in a wide variety of colors, are extremely popular with hummers.

PHLOX PANICULATA
Phlox

Phlox (*Phlox paniculata*) is an old-fashioned flower that is a favorite in the ornamental garden, and has the bonus of attracting hummers. The flowers come in red, pink, lavender, and white. A hardy perennial that grows from Zones 3 to 9, it thrives in full sun.

SALVIA SPP.
Salvias

Many salvias (*Salvia* spp.) are popular with hummingbirds—species and cultivars with red blooms are the best attractors. Hardiness of this perennial varies from Zones 5 to 10 depending on the species, but many native to warmer climes can be grown as annuals in cold-winter areas.

SALVIA ELEGANS
Pineapple sage

Pineapple sage (*Salvia elegans*) is a shrubby perennial with bright red tubular blooms that hummingbirds flock to. While it is hardy only in warm climates (Zones 8 to 10), it may be grown as an annual further north.

TITHONIA ROTUNDIFOLIA
Tithonia

Tithonia (*Tithonia rotundifolia*) is a large, bushy annual (all zones) that bears reddish orange flowers at summer's end.

Opposite: **Penstemon**
(*Penstemon* **'Chester Scarlet'**)

Right: **Phlox**
(*Phlox paniculata* **'Mary Fox'**)

Planting a good selection of trees, shrubs, and flowers that birds like will give you an excellent start in attracting these fluttering creatures to your garden. Make sure to plant with your own tastes in mind, too, for a garden that you and your human guests will enjoy as well as the birds.

Left: **Rich in texture and form, this peaceful woodland garden filled with mature trees, yellow primulas (*Primula bulleyana*), and male fern (*Dryopteris felix-mas*) offers plentiful hiding places, nesting spots, and food sources for a variety of birds.**

ELEMENTS FOR

LURING BIRDS

Left: A small birdhouse is set within the
sheltering growth of a clematis vine.
Above: An eastern bluebird perches
at the edge of a bird table.

irds are such fascinating creatures that attracting them has become something of a science, and producing birdhouses, nest boxes, feeders, birdbaths, and other bird-friendly garden furnishings has become a cottage industry. There are several companies that specialize in bird accoutrements (see Resources on page 121), and nearly every gardening catalog, nursery, and garden center has a section devoted to these elements.

But not all birdhouses, birdbaths, and other such pieces will attract birds successfully, and some may even be dangerous for birds to use. In this chapter we'll take a closer look at the elements you can add to your garden to attract birds and suggest some things you can do to make your additions healthy for birds.

BATHTIME FOR THE BIRDS

Birds will use almost anything that contains enough water for a bath, but with just a little work you can make bathing safer for them. Remember that a wet bird doesn't fly too well, and so will be an easy target for a marauding cat. Make sure that there is a safe perch nearby where birds can dry off and clean their feathers after their bath. Ideally, you will be able to site your birdbath beneath a shade tree but far from shrubs that might shelter a predator. The tree will allow the birds an emergency escape in the event that a cat does attack, while also shielding the bathers from the view of predatory birds. In addition, the shade will help keep the water at a cooler, more pleasant temperature. If your yard has no trees you'll have to make do with an open, sunny site, but realize that this will restrict the types of birds who bathe there to those who feel secure in open spaces.

CHOOSING
THE RIGHT BATH

There are scores of different types of birdbaths available today, and you are certain to find one that suits your taste and your garden's mood. Birdbaths can be found in ceramic, terra-cotta, cast stone or concrete, or plastic, and each of these materials has its advantages and disadvantages. Ceramic, terra-cotta, and stone or concrete are the most ornamental but these may freeze and crack during cold winter weather unless the water inside is kept constantly heated with an electric birdbath heater. Plastic is unlikely to break from freezing (though it sometimes becomes brittle if left exposed for long periods of time), and has the added bonus of being lightweight, but tends to be less attractive.

The traditional shallow basin set atop a pedestal is a good choice for a birdbath, but you needn't limit yourself to this design. Any shallow dish will work just fine—the clay saucers intended for use beneath planters make superb birdbaths. You do need to make sure that the bottom surface of the bath is not too slippery. If you are concerned that it's too slick, the problem can be easily remedied. Simply set a flat, rough stone on the bottom to give the birds better footing.

Many birds adapted for land living avoid deep water, as they can drown quite easily. Their small, twig-like feet are not designed for swimming, so they tend to gravitate to shallow puddles or brooks. The ideal birdbath will have graduated depths, with the

water only about half an inch (1.3cm) deep at the edges and no more than three inches (7.7cm) deep at its greatest depth. This way, small birds will be able to bathe comfortably, as well as larger birds.

For a more natural-looking bath, you might choose a hollowed stone set on the ground. This sort of feature is perfect for woodland spaces or for wilderness-inspired gardens.

Birds will also visit and bathe in a shallow garden pool or slow-running stream, so if you have a water feature in your yard, you may not need to do much else.

A mister or dripper, available from bird supply or specialty gardening stores and catalogs, will get even more attention from the birds.

Above: **Birds, like this Say's phoebe, appreciate supplemental water, especially in arid regions or when water is scarce, such as in deep winter or times of drought.**
Opposite: **Birdbaths are available in a range of shapes, sizes, colors, and materials. This ceramic example is a beautiful garden accent as well as a functional birdbath. If you choose a ceramic bath, do make sure that the bottom is not too slippery.**

WINTER BATHING

Birds like to bathe even in winter, and you can draw winged visitors to your garden in the cold weather by installing an electric heater in your birdbath. These heaters are widely available at pet-supply stores and through specialty catalogs (see Sources on page 121), and are incredibly easy to use. In most cases, you need only set the heater in the bath and plug it in. If your outdoor electrical outlet is far from your birdbath, you'll need to invest in a sturdy outdoor extension cord. Alternatively, you could move your bath a bit closer to the house for the winter months. If you are not going to heat your birdbath water, be sure to empty the basin and store the birdbath indoors for the winter, unless you live in a warm climate. Many birdbath materials are susceptible to cracks and breakage through repeated freezing and thawing, and you'll want to spare yourself the expense of replacing your bath every year.

MAINTAINING THE BIRDBATH

Keep your birdbath pristine by cleaning it out and refilling it with fresh water every day. Birdbaths filled with dirt and debris will soon also be filled with algae and harmful bacteria, and birds know to keep away from such dangers. Make sure to site your birdbath so that routine maintenance tasks are convenient; otherwise, you'll find yourself neglecting this important step and your visitors will stop coming. Put the birdbath within easy reach of the hose and keep a small scrub brush handy. Every few weeks, you'll need to clean the birdbath with bleach or a

SETTING THE TABLE

commercial cleanser to get rid of any dirty buildup. Do be sure, before refilling the basin, that you've thoroughly rinsed off all cleanser residue. You might also try cleaning the bath with a solution of water and white vinegar—this will keep the birdbath clean and is less harsh than bleach.

Be kind to yourself, and place birdbaths at least 5 feet (1.5m) away from bird feeders. Some of our feathered friends are messy eaters, and if you position your birdbath in close proximity to food, you'll find the water full of leftovers and bird droppings, complicating your cleaning chores. Putting the birdbath within visual distance of a feeder, however, will ensure that birds notice it.

A selection of food-producing trees, flowers, and shrubs growing in the landscape is best for the birds, but there may be times you'll want to supplement your garden's offerings with seeds or other food set out in bird feeders. Filling your feeders will ensure that seed-loving birds visit often and are cared for through winter or when times are hard. Wild bird seed mixes are widely available, and will generally include several types of sunflowers, millet, buckwheat, and a tiny seed called canary seed. While some birds are perfectly happy with this mix, others are more choosy, and will discard the seeds they don't

Above: **In the midst of a summer border, a bird table filled with seed and inhabited by two carved ornamental doves awaits its feathered guests.**

Opposite: **A gently splashing fountain is guaranteed to attract birds, who hear the sound and understand that water is nearby. A mister or a drip bottle rigged above a birdbath will have the same powerful effect.**

Above: **The roofed platform feeder in this wild but well-tended garden is sure to attract birds throughout the year but especially in winter, when other foodstuffs may be scarce.**

like, scattering them on the ground about the feeder.

Some gardeners stop feeding birds when winter is over and plants begin providing enough nutrition (and, indeed, many birds lose interest in store-bought seed when better pickin's come along), while other bird lovers continue to set out treats all year long. Whatever you choose to do, there are a few bird-feeding dos and don'ts that you should be aware of. This chapter will help you learn which feeders are best for your needs and where to put your feeder so that birds can eat safely.

To get the most joy out of your bird feeder, site it where you'll be able to watch the birds easily. Depending on your climate and your habits, this might mean placing your feeder in view of a window, where you can relax in comfort and watch the antics of your feathered visitors. Or you might choose to site your feeder where you can enjoy it from a favorite lawn chair, outdoors and at one with the garden.

The ideal situation is to set up several feeders, which will attract an array of different birds. In addition to giving you more opportunities for good viewing, installing a couple of feeders means that you can provide for more birds. When only one feeder is available, the larger, more aggressive birds may outcompete the smaller, more timid ones for the much-desired food. If other feeders are present and there is enough food to go around, the more bashful birds can visit without being chased by the bullies. You might choose cracked corn, which tends to draw ground-feeding birds. Thistle seed (also sold as niger seed) is relatively expensive, but is favored by the much-sought-after goldfinches. Because this seed is fine, you'll need to use a special thistle seed feeder. Peanuts are easy to come by, and are beloved by titmice, jays, and chickadees. See the chart on page 74 to find out more about birds' seed preferences.

Far left: **Indigo buntings have a varied diet that includes insects and seeds. They especially like white millet, which will lure them to feeders.**

Left: **Red-winged blackbird males are common sights at feeders in summer, where they especially savor sunflower seeds.**

Note that some birds feed on the ground, and will scratch in the dust around a bird feeder for fallen seeds. These birds are particularly vulnerable to cats, so if you have cats roaming your neighborhood, make sure there are no shrubs or dense plantings that could conceal cats near your feeder. This way, ground-feeding birds will have warning if a cat approaches and will have a chance to fly to safety.

WHICH FOOD FOR WHICH BIRD?

Birds have their own favorite foods, which will have them flocking to your feeders. Following is a chart of some of these preferred treats and the birds they'll attract.

TREAT	BIRD ATTRACTED
Peanut butter and chopped nut meats	Blue jay, cardinal, catbird, chickadee, finch, grosbeak, nuthatch, titmouse, woodpecker, sparrow
Suet	Brown creeper, chickadee, blue jay, golden- and ruby-crowned kinglet, flicker, red- and white-breasted nuthatch, red-winged blackbird, titmouse, woodpecker
Sunflower seeds	Blue jay, cardinal, chickadee, crossbill, goldfinch, evening grosbeak, mourning dove, purple finch, siskin, white-crowned sparrow, titmouse
Small mixed seed	Brown thrasher, cardinal, catbird, American goldfinch, hermit thrush, horned lark, house finch, junco, mourning dove, pine siskin, evening and pine grosbeak, purple finch, redwing, scrub jay, snow bunting, sparrow, titmouse.
Large seed (kernel corn, oats, rye, wheat, etc.)	Blue grosbeak, blue jay, meadowlark, mourning dove, pheasant, quail, ruffed grouse, woodpecker
Chopped fruit (apple, apricot, banana, blueberry, cherry, cranberry, fig, peach, raisin, strawberry, etc.)	Baltimore oriole, bluebird, catbird, cedar waxwing, hermit thrush, mockingbird, myrtle warbler, robin, thrasher, woodpecker

BIRDS NEED CALCIUM, TOO

Just like people, birds need minerals in order to remain healthy, and the females require additional calcium during breeding season, when they are producing eggs. Birds also ingest grit and tiny stones, which aid them in grinding up their food. You can provide your resident birds with these supplements by offering ground oyster shells, sand, or old building mortar in a shallow container near your feeder.

DIFFERENT KINDS OF FEEDERS

There is a vast range of bird feeders on the market, from simple wooden trays to elaborate reproductions of landmark buildings. There are feeders to suit every type of bird and to catch every gardener's fancy as well. Some are highly ornamental, while others' virtues are chiefly functional. All feeders do have one thing in common, however: all require care and attention from the gardener. Wet seed soon becomes spoiled with mold, while an unstocked feeder disappoints birds, who may stop visiting. An even bigger problem faces those who use feeders that are fully open to the birds, for here bird feces can collect, leading to a proliferation of bacteria.

A well-designed feeder and careful maintenance will help solve many of these problems. Following is a description of the main types of feeders and the specific advantages and disadvantages of each. All feeders should be checked daily to be certain that clean, dry food is available. Feeders should regularly be emptied of their contents and cleaned with a 10 percent bleach solution to disinfect them.

PLATFORM FEEDERS

Platform feeders are simply flat trays with a slightly raised edge, which prevents seed from spilling over the side or blowing away. This type of feeder is highly visible to birds, and will begin attracting them right away. Remember that a larger tray will attract more birds without fear of crowding. You can install a platform feeder at any number of heights—a feeder set

Below: **A Carolina chickadee peruses the offerings at a platform feeder, sometimes called a bird table.**

HOPPER FEEDERS

only a few inches above the earth will be a magnet for ground-feeding birds. Other birds will be nervous feeding on the ground, and will be happier with a platform installed a few feet from the ground.

Platform feeders can be stocked with any type of seed or seed mix, as well as with fruit or suet. Some gardeners even set mealworms out on platform feeders to attract insect-eating birds.

The main disadvantage of platform feeders is that they are open to the sky, and thus the seed gets wet when it rains. Make sure your platform feeders feature plenty of drainage holes, and clean them thoroughly whenever they get wet, as damp, moldy seed will be rejected by the birds.

This type of feeder has a roof, a decided advantage in keeping foods dry and free from birds' bodily wastes and other debris. The sides are usually made of clear plastic, but may be constructed of some other material, such as wood. The seeds fall down through a small gap between the walls and the feeder's floor, and the birds reach the food through this opening. Hopper feeders that feature attached perches are best, since the birds will not be able to soil the seed with droppings. Wide troughs below the gap means that there will be a need for frequent cleanings. You'll also want to be sure that the gap between walls and floors is narrow, or small birds may go in through the opening and be trapped.

Right: **This hopper feeder features attached suet cages, dramatically increasing the varieties of birds you can attract. A red-bellied woodpecker proves the effectiveness of the suet offering.**

BEWARE OF SALMONELLA

There are more than two thousand strains of salmonella bacteria, and periodically outbreaks of salmonellosis occur among wild songbirds. A bird infected with salmonella may appear inactive, sitting with its head under its wing for long periods of time. As the illness spreads throughout the body, the bird may stagger when it walks or shiver uncontrollably, and eventually die.

Birds under stress are most at risk for the disease, so help your feathered friends by providing them with healthy living conditions. Shelter during harsh weather and a plentiful supply of fresh food and water will help birds fight off the bacteria. And not all birds who contract the disease die of it; some remain healthy, though they may still pass the bacteria on to other birds.

The salmonella bacteria is spread to birds by contact with infected birds or by feeding or drinking from contaminated sources. Feeder trays and birdbaths are vulnerable to contamination, as birds are likely to defecate in the seed or water as they eat or bathe. Other animals, such as mice, rats, raccoons, and so on, may also spread the disease. Take the following precautions, particularly if you hear of a local outbreak or have noticed sick or dead birds in your neighborhood.

1. Clean your feeders and birdbath rigorously and frequently, using a 10 percent bleach solution. This is most important if you are using a feeder that is open to the birds. Tube feeders and hopper feeders with perches are the safest, while platform feeders and hopper feeders with large troughs are the most vulnerable to contamination.

2. If you are using one of the more susceptible feeders, such as platform feeders or hopper feeders where the birds can get into the seed, replace food daily; put out only as much food as you think the birds will eat each day, then monitor closely and adjust the amount as necessary.

3. Clean and refill the birdbath every day. Remember that birds drink and bathe from the same source, so water can prove an efficient vehicle for the bacteria.

4. Make sure that stored birdseed is safe from mice and other animal pests, who may spread the bacteria to the food even before you fill the bird feeder.

Finally, be careful when cleaning your feeders and birdbath or disposing of dead birds. While many strains of salmonella are harmful only to certain animals, others may be spread between species, including humans. Don't take any chances that you, your family, or your pets will become infected through contact with sick birds or contaminated bird stations. Use rubber gloves, and keep pets and children safely out of the way. When you are through with your chores, wash or discard anything (such as buckets, scrub brushes, sponges, and so on) that may have come in contact with bird or animal droppings, then wash your hands thoroughly.

Right: **American goldfinches and pine siskins dine heartily at a tube feeder.**

Far right: **Suet offers birds nutritious fats, which they particularly need in cold weather. The tufted titmouse and chickadee shown here are but a few of the birds who will flock to a suet feeder; others include woodpeckers, mockingbirds, nuthatches, and starlings.**

TUBE FEEDERS

Tube feeders are generally made of plastic, and, like hopper feeders, have openings through which the birds can get at seed. The dining birds rest on perches attached near the openings, so the food will not become contaminated with bird feces. If you look for a model with a tight-fitting waterproof lid, the seed should remain dry and fresh.

Tube feeders are popular with certain birds, such as titmice, siskins, and finches. This type of feeder may not attract as many birds, but it does protect seed from rainstorms.

SUET CAGES

Suet is almost always provided in a special cage-style feeder, or occasionally in plastic mesh bags, because it is such a treat that birds will abscond with it and carry it away to a tree where they can eat it out of view. The cage protects the suet from thievery by just one bird, allowing a multitude to enjoy the offering. Both suet cages and cakes of commercially prepared suet are available from specialty stores and mail-order sources (see Sources on page 121). Alternatively, you can prepare your own suet.

PREPARING SUET

Bird suet is basically beef, sheep, or deer fat taken from the area around the animal's kidneys. This area produces a much firmer fat than other areas. The very best suet for birds is made from beef kidney fat. Try asking in a butcher shop for some. It might also be available at your local supermarket meat counter if you ask. If possible, have the butcher grind it. Suet used to be supplied free, but most establishments now charge for it. Primarily a cold-weather treat, fresh suet spoils quickly in warm weather. Once spoiled, it loses nutritive value and birds will not touch it. If you do use suet, place it in a shady area to retard spoilage.

RECIPE FOR A SUET TREAT

To make your own suet concoction, place ground or finely chopped suet in the top of a double boiler. After it melts, allow to cool until hard. Remelt. Add one or more of the following: sunflower seeds, raisins, cracked corn, yellow cornmeal, stale bread crumbs, peanut butter (preferably crunchy), and/or regular oatmeal. Stir well. This recipe makes a fine, firm suet for the birds.

Above: **A red-breasted nuthatch enjoys the offerings at a feeder. These busy little birds will flock to suet feeders, and also like sunflower seeds and chopped nuts.**

MAKING YOUR OWN HUMMINGBIRD NECTAR

Making nectar for your hummingbird feeder is both easy and inexpensive. It can even be better for the birds than a commercially prepared nectar, as many of these have food coloring or preservatives that may be unhealthful. All you need to do is mix up a concoction of four parts water to one part sugar. Boiling the water is a good idea because it makes the sugar dissolve more easily, though you'll then need to wait for it to cool before filling the feeder. Superfine sugar will dissolve readily even in cold water, but you'll find it much pricier than regular granulated sugar.

Never ever substitute honey as the sweetener—it can lead to a fungal disease that is fatal to hummingbirds. Red food coloring, which is sometimes mixed into nectar recipes, should also be avoided because it, too, can be unhealthy for the hummers. The color and shape of the feeder should be more than enough to cue the hummingbirds to the ready source of food.

Above: **A rufous hummingbird sips at the sugar water that will give him the energy to keep buzzing about throughout the day. The yellow "bee guard" keeps flying insects out of the nectar.**

Below right: **Choose a bright red nectar feeder—hummingbirds respond best to this vibrant shade.**

NECTAR FEEDERS

Hummingbird feeders are sure to attract these delightful little birds to your outdoor space. If possible, choose a bright red one with several flower-shaped feeding ports. If you can't find one of this design, do try to make sure that it has the bright red coloring so attractive to these little birds. A good hummingbird feeder will have a "bee guard," a small screen that covers the port and keeps bees and wasps out of the nectar, but allows hummers' bills to get at the concoction. You'll want to make sure that the feeder you buy is easy to clean, as the instant nectar or sugar water you use to fill the feeder is subject to mold, which is bad for the hummingbirds. Clean the feeder often, and refill it regularly.

FRUIT FEEDERS

Fruit feeders are mainly intended to attract orioles, and chiefly consist of a short spike upon which a half an orange (or another piece of fruit) may be impaled. The fancier models may have roofs and perches, but the birds don't require this. You can simply spear a fruit piece at the end of a bare tree branch, or construct a simple fruit feeder from a long nail driven through a piece of wood. Do be sure to affix the feeder at a height where the nail will not injure children or anyone else who might happen by.

Left: **A summer tanager treats himself to a taste of orange. Orioles and tanagers are the birds most likely to visit your fruit feeders, but other species may surprise you.**

CREATING A DIVERSION

Inevitably, your bird-feeding endeavors will attract some birds you'd rather not see, and often these same birds will drive away the shy little birds you are trying so hard to draw. There are a number of ways to discourage large, aggressive birds, and perhaps the fairest and most humane of these methods is the diversion feeder. In this tactic, the undesirables are given their very own feeders full of their favorite foods, which lure them away from your other feeders. Make sure to site your diversion feeder away from your other feeders, but note that there are some cross-preferences, and you may send some of the birds you want to watch off to the diversion feeders as well. The following chart recommends good fillers for your diversion feeders.

BIRD	RECOMMENDED DIVERSION FEEDER FILLER
Blackbird	Old baked goods
Blue jay	Striped sunflower seeds, peanuts, crushed eggshells
House sparrow	Corn, millet, wheat, oats
Mockingbird	Fruit, suet, peanut butter, old bread
Pigeon	Cracked corn, old baked goods, low-cost seed mix
Starling	Suet

WHICH FEEDER FOR WHICH BIRD?

In addition to having their preferred foods, some birds have favorite types of feeders. This chart will help you decide which feeder option is most likely to attract the types of birds you'd like to have in your backyard.

FEEDER TYPE	BIRD ATTRACTED
Tube feeder	American goldfinch, black-capped chickadee, house finch, linnet, tufted titmouse, goldfinch, pine siskin, purple finch, sparrow, and other small seed eaters
Hopper feeder	Blue jay, cardinal, evening grosbeak, house finch, jay, mourning dove, pine siskin, purple finch, and others
Platform feeder (used for fruit and suet in addition to seed)	Bunting, cardinal, catbird, chickadee, flicker, goldfinch, jay, junco, mockingbird, Northern oriole, nuthatch, pine siskin, red-winged blackbird, sapsucker, scarlet tanager, sparrow, thrush, towhee, tufted titmouse, woodpecker
Hummingbird feeder	Hummingbird, Northern oriole, nuthatch, sparrow, tanager, thrush, titmouse, and warbler.
Suet feeder	Flicker, nuthatch, sapsucker, woodpecker

Opposite: **House finches dine at a squirrel-proof feeder—the plastic half-sphere atop the feeder is designed to send squirrels who jump onto it skittering to the ground.**

Below: **Platform feeders are among the simplest to build, and are visited by a number of different species, including the northern cardinal spotted here.**

DEALING WITH SQUIRRELS

Squirrels are devilishly clever, and are ingenious at finding their way into bird feeders. If you hang a feeder from a tree, you are basically providing the neighborhood squirrels with a birdseed free-for-all. In addition to gobbling up all your valuable seed, they are likely to destroy the feeder by gnawing at it to get the treats inside.

Freestanding poles located a safe distance at least 10 feet (3m) from trees or other vertical surfaces and well off the ground (squirrels are expert jumpers) are better options, but even these aren't squirrel-proof. The furry fellows can scramble up even smooth metal poles, though metal will present a greater challenge than the more aesthetically pleasing wooden posts. In the past, some experts recommended greasing the poles with petroleum jelly spiked with cayenne pepper, but this solution has fallen out of favor, as birds' feathers can be coated with the grease, inhibiting their ability to fly. In addition, the effectiveness of the greased pole is usually woefully short-lived, as the squirrels soon figure out how to surmount this obstacle.

The best way to deter squirrels and other pesky mammals such as raccoons and opossums is to install a "baffle" on the bird feeder's pole. A baffle is a conical device that affixes to the pole and prevents animals from climbing all the way up to the feeder. For a baffle to be effective, it must be installed far enough off the ground so that animals cannot simply jump onto the pole above the baffle (five feet [1.5m] should be sufficient). Baffles are generally made of metal or heavy plastic—make sure, if you are purchasing a plastic one, that it is gnaw-proof.

Some hanging feeders are touted as squirrel-proof, and these indeed make it more difficult, if not impossible, for the squirrels to purloin seed. Some tube feeders are equipped with a metal casing that slides down over the tube when anything as heavy as a squirrel lands on the feeder. Others feature metal lips surrounding the seed ports, protecting the heavy-duty plastic from gnawing teeth. Squirrel-proof feeders and baffles can be purchased at specialty garden stores or through the mail from birding or garden catalog companies (see Sources on page 121).

Right: **Tree swallows readily accept nest boxes as their homes, and have been known to return to the same garden year after year to raise their young in the same protected spot.**

A HOME FOR THE BIRDS

Birds that normally nest in cavities, such as blue-birds, chickadees, house wrens, woodpeckers, and many other species, can be encouraged to set up res-idence in a birdhouse or nest box. Nest boxes are typ-ically simple, rectangular affairs with the no-non-sense intent of providing homes for nesting pairs. Birdhouses tend to be shaped more like peoples' houses and are perhaps more ornamental, but good ones have the same straightforward functionality as nest boxes. Both may also be used by birds as winter shelter. Special roosting boxes (which have their holes in the floor) are also available for this purpose. You can purchase ready-made birdhouses and nest boxes from garden suppliers or pet supply stores, or you can make your own.

Unfortunately for the backyard birder, the matter is not as simple as just installing a birdhouse. Different species have exacting requirements, and will reject a house that does not suit their needs precisely. Even more horrifyingly, a bird that unwit-tingly chooses a house that is not safe may suffer for it—for instance, some plastic or ceramic houses or houses with metal roofs have been known to "cook" young birds once the high heat of summer arrives.

Ideally, birdhouses and nest boxes should be made of wood—remember that this is the material that cavity-nesting birds are accustomed to in nature. Every birdhouse needs several ventilation holes (in addition to the entrance hole), to allow heat to escape and fresh air to circulate. Look for a house

that has about three vents on each side, or drill holes there yourself. In addition, you'll need several drainage holes in the floor of the house to let rainwater run out.

The size of the entrance hole and the overall dimensions of the birdhouse are among the most

important factors in making the dwelling satisfactory to nesting pairs. Each species has its own preferences, so don't expect to draw a wide variety of birds with the same house. A bird should fill the entrance to its house, that is, the hole should not allow in anything bigger than the bird. The entrance hole

Above: **A tunnel of chicken wire serves as a predator guard for this weathered nest box. The birds can easily fly through to the house, but the house's contents are out of a cat's arm-reach.**

85

need not have a perch below it; these are completely unnecessary for the birds, who fly right to the entrance edge anyway. And perches make the job of predators much easier, as they have something to grip as they attempt their attack on the nest. (See the sidebar Which House for Which Bird? to find out the best dwelling for the birds you want to attract.)

Birds feel as strongly about the proper height for their houses as they do about other home matters, so it's important to place the right house at the right height for the species you want to attract. Five feet (1.5m) seems to be a popular requirement, and is appropriate for such popular backyard birds as chickadees, bluebirds, nuthatches, titmice, wrens, and tree swallows. Remember that a healthy dose of experimentation is the key to successfully attracting birds. If, after a few weeks, your house remains unoccupied, try moving it up a bit.

WHICH HOUSE FOR WHICH BIRD?

Species	Floor Dimensions	Depth	Entrance Hole Diameter	Entrance Height from Floor	Height Above Ground
Barn owl	10″ × 18″	15″–18″	6″	4″	12′–18′
Bluebird (Eastern)	5″ × 5″	8″	1 ½″	6″	5′
Chickadee	4″ × 4″	8″–10″	1 ⅛″	6″–8″	4′–15′
Carolina wren	4″ × 4″	6″–8″	1 ½″	1″–6″	6′–10′
House wren	4″ × 4″	8″–10″	1 ¼″	1″–6″	6′–10′
Northern flicker	7″ × 7″	16″–18″	2 ½″	14″–16″	6′–20′
Screech owl	8″ × 8″	12″–15″	3″	9″–12″	10′–30′

Below: **Don't crowd birdhouses into your garden—most birds are territorial and won't nest close to other birds.**

Never ever paint the inside of your birdhouse. If you want to paint or stain the outside of the house, be sure to purchase a water-based exterior paint or stain. Wood preservatives are generally ill-advised, but you may be able to find one of a few that the Environmental Protection Agency (EPA) has approved for use with animals and plants: look for Cuprinol wood preservative clear #20 or green #10.

BIRDS NEED SPACE

Very few birds will nest in crowded conditions. Typically, the houses must be located 200 or 300 feet (60.9 or 91.4m) apart, depending on the species. This means that the average suburban backyard, which is about ¼ acre (0.1ha), can support only one or two birdhouses. If you are lucky enough to have more land, go ahead and set up more houses. Some

birds, most notably martins, will nest in "bird condos," the houses with several living spaces within the same building. This may be a good solution if you want lots of nesting birds but have a small garden.

Note that birds gravitate most to houses situated in the sun. This is not so difficult to arrange if you are planning on affixing the house to a free-standing post, but is considerably more tricky if you want to install your house on the trunk of a tree. Observe the tree where you plan to put the birdhouse, and make sure that the front of the house will get at least six hours of sun each day. In addition, the house should be sited so that howling winds and the rains they bring will not squall through the entrance hole. If your yard is subject to prevailing winds, try to locate your house so that the back of the structure is generally to the wind. Whether you are attaching the house to a tree or to a post, be certain to affix it securely, using rust-proof nails. Birds don't like rickety, swaying houses any more than people do.

If you have lots of marauding predators in your neighborhood, you may need to take extra precautions to keep them away. Once you've drawn birds to your birdhouse, stay vigilant for cats and squirrels, and chase them away. With any luck, they'll come to learn that the birdhouse is not worth their time and trouble. A predator guard, a small piece of wood with an entrance hole cut into it, will make the entry passage into the house longer, deterring many nest raiders. If you live in an area that is home to tree snakes, you'll also have to watch out for these— plastic mesh encircling the tree trunk will deter the snakes from reaching their goal.

CARE AND MAINTENANCE

Make sure to clean your birdhouses and nest boxes out after each nesting, as some birds won't choose an untidy box. Once you've removed old nesting material, dust the interior of the house with rotenone (an organic pesticide), which will kill any parasites that might have infested the house. Also check the birdhouses periodically if they are not in use to be sure that debris has not gathered and to confirm that unwelcome residents, such as mice or wasps, have not invaded.

Opposite: **Bluebirds are among the easiest birds to attract to nest boxes in the backyard, because they like the mix of wooded lots and open spaces that most suburbs provide.**

Far Left: **A nest box mounted on a free-standing pole can be positioned in the sunny situation birds like. This box's proximity to a holly bush offers the bonus of nearby cover and, in season, edible berries.**

Left: **Yellow-shafted flickers, like this alert male, will happily choose a nest box for a home. The diameter of the entry hole should be 2 inches (5cm), but these birds aren't fussy about the box's height.**

With some care and attention, you can provide supplemental food and shelter to keep birds happy all year 'round. As you choose the elements you wish to add to your bird garden, remember that you want to create a healthy environment for the birds and a garden that you can enjoy as well. If you overcommit yourself in terms of maintenance, your garden will become a chore rather than a pleasure—something that's good for neither you nor your bird visitors.

Left: Simple yet elegant, this classic pedestal birdbath invites birds to drink and bathe. The accompanying planting is exquisite, but is only safe for birds if the neighborhood is free of roaming cats. Otherwise, leave space around the bath so that birds have warning of approaching predators.

CHAPTER 4

ENJOYING
THE BIRDS

Left: **Dicksissels prefer open spaces,
such as fields and meadows.**
Above: **A common yellowthroat perches
on a single stem.**

There are more than eight hundred species of birds native to North America, so we will touch on the ones most likely to visit your backyard. If you want to learn more about identifying birds and understand the habits of many different species, invest in a good field guide (see Further Reading on page 121). A guide that is geared to your region will be even more detailed than those that cover the entire continent.

Bird feeding is a hobby that is enjoyed by more than 83 million people in North America, and, increasingly, it is a service that may well prove integral to the continued survival of many bird species. Like so many animals, birds face increasing pressures from urban development and destruction of their habitat. Migration routes have been disturbed and breeding grounds devastated by deforestation and real estate development. Recent studies have shown that the populations of songbirds in North America have been steadily declining, and our involvement may be crucial in providing safe places for birds to shelter, feed, and reproduce.

Birdwatching is among the most popular hobbies, and can be lots of fun for the whole family. If you set up your yard optimally, with plenty of bird-feeding stations, a nest box, and many plants that birds flock to, even young children will be able to follow the daily activities of local bird families. Older children will enjoy learning to identify various species and learning the calls, diet, and habits of each. Watching birds is also a good way for parents to teach their children respect for their fellow creatures and a sense of stewardship of the earth.

BE ON THE LOOKOUT

Understanding the places that different birds gravitate toward helps you spot them. This handy guide directs your attention to the habitats most likely to attract certain species of birds.

Forests	Chickadees, grosbeaks, jays, juncos, kinglets, nuthatches, purple finches, ruby-throated hummingbirds, sparrows, tanagers, titmice, thrushes, veery, vireos, warblers, woodpeckers
Meadows and fields	Bluebirds, bobolinks, dicksissels, field sparrows, goldfinches, meadowlarks, quail, swallows, swifts
Areas near houses and barns	Blackbirds, magpies, pigeons, purple martins, robins, swallows, starlings, swifts, wrens
Bogs and swampy areas	Blackbirds, cedar waxwings, grackles, marsh wrens

Opposite: **Introducing feeders and nest boxes to your yard, as well as planting trees, shrubs, and flowers where birds can shelter and feed, helps ensure birds' survival.**

First, make sure to site your bird feeding area where it will be visible from a comfortable chair, as one of the benefits of drawing birds to your yard is that you will be able to watch their daily activities. A pair of binoculars, a field guide, and a notebook are useful accessories to keep near your bird-viewing seat—these tools will help you keep track of your backyard visitors.

Remember that in winter you'll have to get out to your feeder to clean it and add food, so be sure to put it where it will be accessible even when snow is deep. Once you've planted your bird-lover's garden and found a comfortable spot to perch yourself, you are ready to begin enjoying the antics of your resident and visiting birds.

Left: **The western tanager is a shy bird usually found in the treetops of the mountainous West. But look for him at nectar or fruit feeders as well.**

IN YOUR OWN BACKYARD

You shouldn't expect to see every kind of bird in your garden, no matter what you plant or how much birdseed you put out. If your house isn't in the range of a particular species, nothing you do will attract it. Here is a brief guide that will help you identify the bird species you are most likely to see in your own yard, divided by geographical region. Note that some birds do migrate, and so will reside in northern regions during summer and southern regions in winter.

Right: **Wilson's warbler**

NORTH

American redstart

American tree sparrow

American robin

Black-billed magpie

Baltimore oriole

Black-capped chickadee

Black-throated green warbler

Blackpoll warbler

Blue jay

Brewer's blackbird

Brown creeper

Bullock's oriole

Cedar waxwing

Common grackle

Dark-eyed junco

Dicksissel

Downy woodpecker

Eastern bluebird

Eastern meadowlark

Eastern phoebe

Evening grosbeak

Fox sparrow

Golden-crowned kinglet	Gray jay	Indigo bunting
Golden-shafted flicker	Hermit thrush	Lazuli bunting
Goldfinch	House finch	Mourning dove
Gray catbird	House wren	Northern bobwhite
		Ovenbird
		Pine grosbeak
		Pine siskin
		Purple finch
		Purple martin
		Red crossbill
		Red-shafted flicker
		Red-winged blackbird
		Rose-breasted grosbeak
		Ruby-crowned kinglet
		Rusty blackbird
		Scarlet tanager
		Solitary vireo
		Song sparrow
		Swamp sparrow
		Veery
		Warbling vireo
		Western meadowlark
		Western tanager
		White-breasted nuthatch
		White-crowned sparrow
		White-throated sparrow
		White-winged crossbill
		Wilson's warbler
		Winter wren
		Wood thrush
		Yellow warbler

Left: **Eastern bluebird**

SOUTH

American robin	Brown thrasher	Cedar waxwing
Baltimore oriole	Brown-headed nuthatch	Common grackle
Blue grosbeak	Cardinal	Common yellowthroat
Blue jay	Carolina chickadee	Downy woodpecker
Brewer's blackbird	Carolina wren	Eastern bluebird

Right: **Winter wren**

Left: **White-breasted nuthatch**

Eastern meadowlark	Kentucky warbler	Rusty blackbird
Eastern phoebe	Mockingbird	Scarlet tanager
Field sparrow	Mourning dove	Song sparrow
Golden-shafted flicker	Northern bobwhite	Summer tanager
Goldfinch	Painted bunting	Tufted titmouse
Gray catbird	Pine warbler	White-breasted nuthatch
Hairy woodpecker	Purple martin	White-eyed vireo
Hermit thrush	Red-bellied woodpecker	Winter wren
House finch	Red-eyed vireo	Wood thrush
House wren	Red-winged blackbird	Yellow warbler
Indigo bunting	Ruby-throated hummingbird	

EAST

American robin	Blue jay	Common yellowthroat
Baltimore oriole	Cardinal	Downy woodpecker
Black-capped chickadee	Cedar waxwing	Eastern bluebird
Black-throated green warbler	Common grackle	Eastern meadowlark

Right: **Mourning dove**

Eastern phoebe

Field sparrow

Golden-shafted flicker

Goldfinch

Gray catbird

Hermit thrush

House finch

House wren

Indigo bunting

Kentucky warbler

Mockingbird

Mourning dove

Northern bobwhite

Ovenbird

Purple martin

Red-bellied woodpecker

Red-eyed vireo

Red-winged blackbird

Rose-breasted grosbeak

Ruby-throated hummingbird

Scarlet tanager

Song sparrow

Swamp sparrow

Tufted titmouse

Veery

White-breasted nuthatch

White-eyed vireo

Wood thrush

Yellow warbler

Left: **Blue jay**

Right: **Rose-breasted grosbeak**

MIDWEST

American robin

Baltimore oriole

Bell's vireo

Bewick's wren

Black-capped chickadee

Black-headed grosbeak

Blue grosbeak

Blue jay

Brewer's blackbird

Cardinal

Carolina chickadee

Carolina wren

Cedar waxwing

Common yellowthroat

Common grackle

Dicksissel

Downy woodpecker

Eastern bluebird

Eastern meadowlark

Eastern phoebe

Field sparrow

Golden-shafted flicker

Goldfinch

Grasshopper sparrow

Gray catbird

House finch

House wren

Indigo bunting

Kentucky warbler

Lark bunting

Left: **Kentucky warbler**

Lazuli bunting	Red-winged blackbird	Warbling vireo
Mockingbird	Rose-breasted grosbeak	Western meadowlark
Mourning dove	Ruby-throated hummingbird	Western tanager
Northern bobwhite	Say's phoebe	White-breasted nuthatch
Ovenbird	Scarlet tanager	White-eyed vireo
Painted bunting	Song sparrow	Wood thrush
Purple martin	Summer tanager	Yellow warbler
Red-bellied woodpecker	Swamp sparrow	Yellow-headed blackbird
Red-shafted flicker	Tufted titmouse	

WEST

Acorn woodpecker	Brewer's blackbird	Common yellowthroat
American goldfinch	Brewer's sparrow	Costa's hummingbird
American robin	Brindled titmouse	Dark-eyed junco
Anna's hummingbird	Bullock's oriole	Downy woodpecker
Bell's vireo	Bush tit	Evening grosbeak
Bewick's wren	Cactus wren	Fox sparrow
Black phoebe	California quail	Gambel's quail
Black-capped chickadee	Cardinal	Golden-crowned kinglet
Black-headed grosbeak	Carolina chickadee	Golden-crowned sparrow
Black-throated sparrow	Cedar waxwing	Gray catbird
Blue grosbeak	Common grackle	Great-tailed grackle

Right: **Purple finch**

Orange-crowned warbler

Ovenbird

Pine grosbeak

Pine sisken

Pinyon jay

Plain titmouse

Purple finch

Purple martin

Pygmy nuthatch

Red-breasted nuthatch

Red-shafted flicker

Red-winged blackbird

Rosy finch

Ruby-crowned kinglet

Sage thrasher

Say's phoebe

Scaled quail

Scott's oriole

Scrub jay

Solitary vireo

Song sparrow

Stellar's jay

Summer tanager

Warbling vireo

Western bluebird

Western meadowlark

Western tanager

White-breasted nuthatch

Winter wren

Yellow warbler

Yellow-headed blackbird

Hermit thrush

House finch

House wren

Lazuli bunting

Lesser goldfinch

Magpie

Mockingbird

Mountain bluebird

Mountain chickadee

Mourning dove

Left: **Dark-eyed junco**

THE MATING GAME

We are all familiar with certain bird behaviors, and many of these can be viewed easily as birds choose mates, nest, and raise their families all in close proximity to our own families.

Hearing birdsong filling the trees is a thrilling experience that most of us have shared, but understanding the reasons birds do what they do can greatly enhance your appreciation of these colorful garden guests. Singing, for example, generally means that an adult male is trying to attract a mate (though there are species in which both sexes sing). Alternatively, it may indicate that he is defending his territory. Most birds sing while perched, but others, such as the skylark, sing on the wing.

If you've ever taken a walk with an experienced birder, you know that songs and calls identify the bird even when it's hidden in the trees. It takes a bit of practice to associate the songs with birds, but it's fun to learn. As you sit in your garden, close your eyes and focus on the sounds you hear. Gradually begin to filter out all but the bird calls and songs. A good field guide will help you match the calls you hear with the birds you see. You will also find it helpful to listen to cassette tapes or compact discs with recordings of various birdsongs; many commercial birding tapes are available. You might also choose to record some local birdsongs yourself and use these to become familiar with the sounds of birds in your region.

In addition to singing, birds use a variety of methods to attract a mate. Among the most famous examples are the complex and elegant mating dances performed by swans and cranes. Plumage displays, such as those executed by peacocks, and other transformations, such as neck pouch swellings, are other types of courtship ritual.

Still other birds perform their courtship dances while in flight, swooping and turning in elaborate patterns in the air. Male hummingbirds are among those you may watch as they display in midair, showing off their brightly colored plumage to admiring females.

Some birds defend a territory, with the female choosing both the mate and the spot she wants to breed at the same time. Still other species establish communal mating grounds, called leks, and a female, attracted by the calls of the males, chooses among the males gathered there.

Right: **An eastern meadowlark male defends his territory vigorously by singing. If another male meadowlark trespasses into his domain, the established male chases his competitor away.**

Left: **House finches are social birds who generaly travel in loose flocks, but in spring they pair off to begin the business of producing the next generation.**

WHO'S DOING WHAT?

Following are some of the courtship behaviors you might expect to see in your garden or in the fields and forests surrounding your home. Many breeding behaviors contain one or more elements of courtship; for example, some birds combine territorial defense and sweet song with ritualized chases of the female, while others sing and display their plumage as well as offer bits of food to the female. Below you'll find some of the most obvious elements of courtship rituals; observe the birds carefully and note the variations in behavior for the different species you see.

Aerial courtship	Anna's hummingbird, eastern bluebird, mourning dove, ruby-throated hummingbird
Song and display	Baltimore oriole, Brewer's blackbird, common flicker, gray catbird, greater roadrunner, scarlet tanager
Territorial defense and calls	American goldfinch, American robin, brown towhee, eastern meadowlark, house wren, indigo bunting, lazuli bunting, mountain chickadee, purple martin, song sparrow, wrentit, yellow warbler

RAISING A FAMILY

Once birds have selected a mate, they are busy with the activities that lead to continuation of the species. Some birds are monogamous and mate for life, establishing strong pair bonds and raising nestful after nestful of hatchlings. Other species stay together for just one breeding season, while still others mate with many partners during one season. These mating habits are most likely genetically determined.

titmice and chickadees, are cavity nesters, and build their homes in existing holes in trees or in holes that they may excavate in partially rotten wood. Cavity nesters are the birds most likely to set up residence in your birdhouses. (See Chapter 3 for more on birdhouses.)

Once the birds have settled into their nests, the female will lay her eggs. Most species lay eggs associated with a particular color, shape, and pattern (think robin's egg blue), but some species lay eggs of several different colors and markings.

The bird parent sits on the eggs to keep them warm, pressing its brood patches (unfeathered skin with a higher temperature than surrounding skin) against the eggs. When a chick is ready to hatch, it begins to chirp within the eggshell and slowly chips away at the shell with its egg tooth, a sharp calcium prominence on its beak.

At birth, the baby birds are either altricial or precocial. Altricial species hatch naked and defenseless, and require much care and attention from their parents. In some species the parents feed their young whole pieces of food from their beaks, while other birds must first process the food and then regurgitate it for the nestlings. Female songbirds are known to lose much of their body weight as they race to and fro trying to keep up with the needs of their demanding offspring.

Precocial species have babies that are much more self-sufficient. These young are born with soft down and can move about and feed themselves soon after they hatch. Some can even fly only days after hatching. The role of parents in precocial species is generally to protect the young from predators

Opposite: **Blue-gray gnatcatcher mates build exquisite, cup-shaped nests together. Once the nest frame is finished, the birds bind lichens to the nest's exterior using the gossamer strands of spider or caterpillar silk as their thread.**

Above: **An American robin sits on her eggs in the safety of a white pine tree.**

The variety of nesting behaviors is probably as vast as the range of courtship behaviors. Birds such as the mourning dove, the robin, and the cardinal construct our typical idea of a bird's nest, with twigs, sticks, and other handy bits woven into the traditional cupped basket shape in the branches of a tree. But the lark bunting builds its nest in a depression on the ground and the Baltimore oriole weaves a spectacular, long pouch that hangs from the ends of several branches. Other birds, such as

Above: **Robins' eggs are among the most widely recognized, due to their signature blue color. Robins typically lay three or four eggs, which will hatch after about two weeks into helpless baby birds.**

(often by pretending to be injured and luring the predator away from the little birds) and to teach the babies what to eat.

By midsummer, the altricial young are learning to fly. This is an exciting time, and if you are lucky, you may be able to watch as the fledglings take their first flying lessons. This is an especially vulnerable time for birds, so be careful to keep cats and other predators away from the area. Overcurious children can also be a hindrance to the birds, so teach your children the importance of leaving the birds in peace.

STAY FAR FROM THE NEST

Do be sure to keep your distance from bird nests. You'll get your best view by using a good pair of binoculars and mustering up some patience. Remember that a bird will sometimes abandon its nest if it fears that predators have discovered it, and keep in mind that humans fall into the category of predators.

BACKYARD FEEDING

As discussed in chapters 2 and 3, you can keep your backyard birds happy and healthy by providing them with natural foods growing in your garden and by supplementing at feeders as appropriate. See these chapters for details about the specific plants and foods to offer. Insect-eating birds will also help you by gobbling up pests such as beetles, weevils, aphids, termites, wasps, cutworms, and others.

Below: **Mockingbird babies grow up quickly, leaving the nest after less than two weeks. This allows their parents to raise several sets of offspring in the same season, as long as food sources are abundant.**

Opposite: **This side yard is arranged optimally for birdwatching. Trees, shrubs, and lush underplantings combine with a functional nest box and several feeders to lure winged visitors, all within view of a big bay window.**

Right: **With patience, you can teach a Carolina chickadee to eat from your hand.**

HAND-FEEDING BIRDS

There is some controversy about whether wild birds should become accustomed to direct contact with people. Clearly, becoming habituated to humans means that some birds may put themselves at risk by approaching people who do not have their best interests at heart. Yet many people enjoy trying to get birds to feed from their hands, and indeed entire books have been devoted to the subject. Remember that this is a project that requires a lot of patience.

You may have noticed that birds come when you put out food. To begin getting your backyard birds to visit on cue, use a specific sound, such as a small bell, each time you put out food. Continue for several weeks.

After the birds begin to come on cue, begin sitting in the vicinity of the feeder after you ring the bell. Sit very still for about fifteen minutes each time, gradually moving your chair closer to the food source.

Once the birds have become used to your presence, empty most of the food tray, leaving some seed in one section. Put some food in your hand and place your hand, opened flat, near the food tray. (Note that some people have had success by first placing an empty glove with food in the palm near the feeder tray.) You must be extremely still and quiet. Do not swallow—swallowing makes the bird think of you as a predator. Do not look at birds that arrive.

Speak in a gentle conversational voice. When a bird finally lands on your hand to feed, do not move and do not attempt to touch the bird. Some bird species are more readily accepting of hand feeding than others. Among these are chickadees, titmice, jays, and, of course, pigeons.

Above: **Varied and healthy plantings grow above and below unmortared stone retaining walls. These walls allow plant seeds to take root between the stones, and offer homes to insects that attract birds.**

As you observe the birds in your garden, you'll see that their range of diet and eating habits is as wide as their other behaviors. Members of the chickadee family are well-known for their acrobatic prowess, often hanging upside down as they forage for insects or seeds. Robins are a familiar sight on lawns, as they search the grass for earthworms and other insects, and eat fruit as well, particularly in winter months when insects are scarce. Summer tanagers can scoop up insects on the wing.

Get to know the birds in your neighborhood, and keep track of their likes and dislikes (a good field guide or a knowledgeable friend can help you identify your backyard visitors). This will help you become a better bird gardener and is an entertaining pastime in and of itself.

A Long, Strange Trip

When summer is over, many species of birds make preparations for the big move to their winter homes. These birds are migrators. As autumn approaches, the migrators store fat reserves that will provide them with the energy they need for their long journey. Some birds' body fat increases from less than 10 percent to between 40 and 50 percent.

The flight south allows migrating birds to avoid the harsh winter weather of colder climates and to find abundant food. The return north in the spring lets them take advantage of the longer spring and summer days, giving them more time to gather food (near the equator, days and nights are of equal length all year 'round). For busy parents and hungry nestlings, these longer days are invaluable to survival.

The precise triggers that start birds on their migrations and the mechanics that allow them to find their way across many thousands of miles are not fully understood. Many birds not only return to the same region where they themselves were hatched, they find the precise location. Researchers believe that birds use the sun and stars to help them navigate. In addition, they have magnetite in neck tissue, which most likely functions as a sort of internal compass.

While most species move in north-south migration patterns, some birds migrate east or west. Others migrate shorter distances, from mountains to lowlands, for instance, or they may fly southward only a short ways. American robins, for example, include southern Canada and the northern United States as the northern edge of their winter range.

Some birds are adapted for cold winter weather, and these are known as residents, since they stay in the same place all year long.

Below: **Most orioles, like this Bullock's oriole, winter in Central and South America.**

Take time out to enjoy the fruits of your labors by relaxing with a glass of iced tea and enjoying your new bird neighbors. You can feel serene in the knowledge that you are helping to preserve a beautiful part of the natural world even as you revel in the retreat you have created for yourself.

Left: **A gardener who incorporates varied habitats—a lawn area, a stone wall, pastel cottage flowers, evergreen shrubs, and beyond, tall grasses and woodland—creates a landscape that is a charming haven for people and birds alike.**

PLANT HARDINESS ZONES

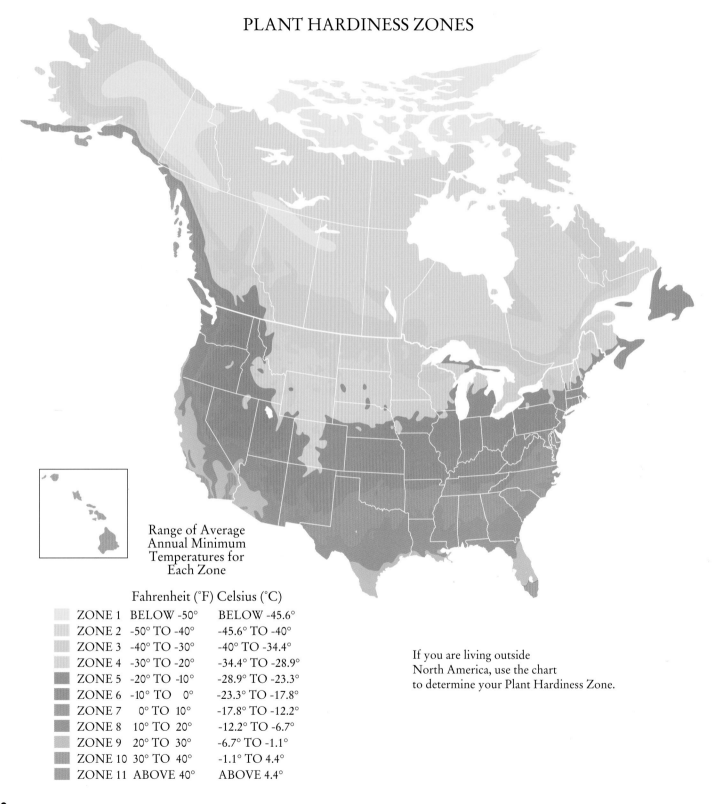

Range of Average
Annual Minimum
Temperatures for
Each Zone

		Fahrenheit (°F)	Celsius (°C)
	ZONE 1	BELOW -50°	BELOW -45.6°
	ZONE 2	-50° TO -40°	-45.6° TO -40°
	ZONE 3	-40° TO -30°	-40° TO -34.4°
	ZONE 4	-30° TO -20°	-34.4° TO -28.9°
	ZONE 5	-20° TO -10°	-28.9° TO -23.3°
	ZONE 6	-10° TO 0°	-23.3° TO -17.8°
	ZONE 7	0° TO 10°	-17.8° TO -12.2°
	ZONE 8	10° TO 20°	-12.2° TO -6.7°
	ZONE 9	20° TO 30°	-6.7° TO -1.1°
	ZONE 10	30° TO 40°	-1.1° TO 4.4°
	ZONE 11	ABOVE 40°	ABOVE 4.4°

If you are living outside
North America, use the chart
to determine your Plant Hardiness Zone.

SOURCES

Appalachian Gardens
PO Box 82
Waynesboro, PA 17268
717-762-4312
Conifers, trees

Beaver Creek Nursery
7526 Pelleaux Road
Knoxville, TN 37938
423-922-3961
Conifers, grasses, trees

Berry Hill Limited
75 Burwell Road
St. Thomas, Ontario
Canada N5P 3R5
800-668-3072
Birdhouses, bird feeders

Bluebird Orchard Nursery
429 East Randall Street
Coopersville, MI 49404
616-837-9598
Fruit, trees

Bluestem Prairie Nursery
RR 2, Box 106-A
Hillsboro, IL 62049
217-532-6344
Grasses, seeds, wildflowers

Bruce Barber Bird Feeders, Inc.
4600 Jason Street
Denver, CO 80211
800-528-2794
Handcrafted birdhouses, bird feeders

Busse Gardens
5973 Oliver Avenue S.W.
Cokato, MN 55321-4229
800-544-3192
Gasses, hostas, perennials, wildflowers

C.C. Chirps Internet Cafe
www.ccchirps.com
360-695-7063
Custom-mixed bird seed

Clifford's Perennials & Vine
 Route 2, Box 320
East Troy, WI 53120
414-968-4040
Perennials, trees, vines

Desertland Nursery
PO Box 26126
El Paso, TX 79926
915-858-1130
Cactus, seeds

Duncraft
PO Box 9020
Penacook, NH 03303-9020
800-593-5656
www.duncraft.com
Birdhouses, baths, feeders, seed mixes and treats, and many more bird fostering accessories

Earthly Goods Ltd.
PO Box 614
New Albany, IN 47150
812-944-3283
Nesting boxes, bird feeders, grasses, wildflowers

Eastern Plant Specialists
Box 226
Georgetown, ME 04548
800-WILL-GRO
Conifers, fruit, perennials, trees, wildflowers

Far North Gardens
PO Box 126
New Hudson, MI 48165
810-486-4203
Grasses, perennials, seeds, wildflowers

Gardeners Eden
PO Box 7307
San Francisco, CA 94120-7307
800-822-9600
Birdbaths, bird feeders

Indiana Berry and Plant Co.
5218 West 500 South
Huntingburg, IN 47542
800-295-2226
Fruit

Johnny's Selected Seeds
Foss Hill Road
Albion, ME 04910-9731
207-437-9294
Grasses, heirloom seeds, herbs

Joy Creek Nursery
20300 N.W. Watson Road
Scappoose, OR 97056
503-543-7474
Grasses, perennials

Kurt Bluemel, Inc.
2740 Greene Lane
Baldwin, MD 21013
410-557-7229
Grasses, perennials, waterscapes

Lazy Hill Fam Designs
PO Box 235
Lazy Hill Road
Colerain, NC 27924
919-356-2040
Birdhouses, feeders, nesting boxes

Living Tree Nursery
PO Box 10082
Berkeley, CA 94709-5082
510-420-1440
Fruit, heirlooms, trees

Mellinger's
2310 West South Range Road
North Lima, OH 44452-9731
800-321-7444
Perennials, wildflowers

Moon Mountain Wildflowers
PO Box 725
Carpinteria, CA 93014
805-684-2565
Seeds, wildflowers

Mostly Natives Nursery
27235 Highway 1, Box 258
Tomales, CA 94971
707-878-20009
Grasses, perennials, trees, wildflowers

Native American Seed
3400 Long Prairie Road
Flower Mound, TX 75028
Grasses, seeds, wildflowers

Native Gardens
5737 Fisher Lane
Greenback, TN 37742
423-856-0220
Grassses, seeds, trees, wildflowers

Natural Gardener's Catalog
8648 Old Bee Caves Road
Austin, TX 78735
800-320-0724
Organics, garden supplies

Nature's Control
PO Box 35
Medford, OR 97501
514-8998318
Organics, garden supplies

Perky-Pet Brand
www.perkypet.com
Wild bird feeders, accessories.

Plants of the Southwest
Agua Fria, Route 6
Box 11-A
Santa Fe, NM 87501
800-788-7333
Grasses, heirlooms, seeds, trees, wildflowers

Prairie Nursery
PO Box 306
Westfield, WI 53964
608-296-3679
Grasses, seeds, wildflowers
Salt Spring Seeds
Box 33
Ganges, British Columbia
V0S 1E0
604-537-5269
Heirlooms, organics, seeds

Seeds of Change
PO Box 15700
Santa Fe, NM 87506
505-438-8080
Heirlooms, organics, seeds

Shepherd's Garden Seeds
6116 Highway 9
Felton, CA 95018
408-335-691-
Heirlooms, herbs, supplies, seeds

Wild Birds Forever
www.birdsforever.com
Bird feeders, birdbath heaters, binoculars, books, ornaments

Wild Birds Unlimited
11711 N. College Ave.
Suite 146
Carmel, IN 46032-5655
800-326-4928 (store locator)
Caters to backyard birdfeeding hobbyists. Visit website or call toll-free to find store locations across the United States and Canada. Website also features internet store.

BIRDING WEBSITES

Birdwatching.com
An informational site about wild birds and the sport of birding. Includes a bookstore and birding gifts.

Birding.com
An informational site for the novice and expert birder.

Peterson Online
www.petersononline.com
Features information on identifying birds. The Bird Watcher's Digest offers articles from the magazine.

FURTHER READING

Adler, Bill. *Outwitting Squirrels: 101 Cunning Stratagems to Reduce Dramatically the Egregious Misappropriation of Seed from Your Birdfeeder by Squirrels.* Chicago Review Press, 1996.

———. *Impeccable Birdfeeding: How to Discourage Scuffling, Hull-Dropping, Seed-Throwing, Unmentionable Nuisances and Vulgar Chatter at Your Birdfeeder.* Chicago Review Press, 1992.

Attenborough, David. *The Life of Birds.* Princeton University Press, 1998.

Baldwin, Edwin A. *Birdfeeders, Shelters and Baths (The Weekend Workshop Collection).* Storey Books, 1990.

———. *Building Birdhouses and Feeders (Ortho Library).* Orthos Books, 1990.

Bull, John, et al. *National Audubon Society Field Guide to North American Birds: Eastern Region.* Knopf, 1994.

Campbell, Scott D. *The Complete Book of Birdhouse Construction for Woodworkers.* Dover Publications, 1989.

———. *Easy-to-Make Bird Feeders for Woodworkers.* Dover Publications, 1989.

Cosgrove, Irene. *My Recipes are for the Birds.* Doubleday. 1999.

Dunn, Jon L. *National Geographic Field Guide to the Birds of North America: Revised and Updated.* National Geographic Society, 1999.

Elliott, Lang and Marie Read. *Common Birds and Their Songs.* Houghton Mifflin Co., 1998.

Garrett, Kimball L., et al. *A Field Guide to Warblers of North America (The Peterson Field Guide Series).* Houghton Mifflin Co., 1997.

Gerhards, Paul. *Birdhouses & Feeders You Can Make: Complete Plans and Instructions for Bird-Friendly Nesting and Feeding Sites.* Stackpole Books, 1999.

Griggs, Jack L. *All the Birds of North America: American Bird Conservancy's Field Guide.* HarperCollins, 1997.

Griggs, Jack L. and Virginia Croft, ed. *All the Backyard Birds: East (American Bird Conservancy Compact Guide).* Harperperennial Library, 1998.

Hart, Rhonda Massingham. *Bird Food Recipes.* Storey Books, 1995.

Kaufman, Kenn. *Lives of North American Birds (Peterson Natural History Companions).* Houghton Mifflin Co., 1996.

MacKenzie, Dave. *Bird Boxes and Feeders for the Garden*. Sterling Publications, 1998.

McCauley, Jane R. *Field Guide to the Birds of North America*. National Geographic Society, 1993

Peterson, Roger Tory, illustrator. *A Field Guide to Western Birds*. Houghton Mifflin Co., 1990.

Peterson, Roger Tory and Virginia Marie Peterson, illustrators. *A Field Guide to the Birds: A Completely New Guide to All the Birds of Eastern and Central North America (Peterson Field Guides)*. Houghton Mifflin Co., 1998.

Ramuz, Mark and Frank Delicata. *Birdhouses: 20 Unique Woodworking Projects for Houses and Feeders*. Storey Books, 1996.

Robbins, Chandler S., et al. *Birds of North America: A Guide to Field Identification*. Golden Books (Adult), 1983.

Sibley, Hi. *Bird Houses, Feeders You Can Make*. Goodheart-Wilcox Co., 1991.

Slinger, Joey. *Down & Dirty Birding: From the Sublime to the Ridiculous—Here's All the Outrageous but True Stuff You Ever Wanted to Know About North American Birds*. Fireside, 1996.

Stokes, Donald and Lillian Stokes. *Stokes Field Guide to Birds: Eastern Region (Stokes Field Guides)*. Little Brown & Co., 1996.

———. *Stokes Field Guide to Birds: Western Region (Stokes Field Guides)*. Little Brown & Co., 1996.

Stokes, Donald W. et al. *The Bird Feeder Book: An Easy Guide to Attracting, Identifying, and Understanding Your Feeder Birds*. Little Brown & Co., 1987.

———. *The Hummingbird Book: The Complete Guide to Attracting, Identifying, and Enjoying*. Little Brown & Co., 1989.

———. *Stokes Field Guide to Bird Songs: Eastern Region*. Time Warner Audio Books, 1997.

Thompson, Bill and Bird Watcher's Digest eds. *Bird Watching for Dummies (1st ed.)*. IDG Books Worldwide, 1997.

Udvardy, Miklos D. F. and John Farrand Jr., *National Audubon Society Field Guide to North American Birds: Western Region*. Knopf, 1994.

Walton, Richard K., ed. and Robert W. Lawson. *Birding by Ear: Eastern/Central (Peterson Field Guides)*. Houghton Mifflin Audio, 1999.

Weidensaul, Scott. *Living on the Wind: Across the Hemisphere With Migratory Birds*. North Point Press, 1999.

Wheye, Darryl, contributor, et al. *The Birder's Handbook: A Field Guide to the Natural History of North American Birds; Including All Species That Regularly Breed North of Mexico*. Fireside, 1988.

INDEX

Abelia grandiflora, 18

Abies spp., 33

Acer campestre, 19

Acer spp., 50

Adam's needle, 49

Agastache spp., 58

Allium schoenoprasum, 36

Alopecurus spp., 50

Amelanchier x grandiflora, 10

Amelancier spp., 51

American arborvitae, 18

American robin, *110*

Andropogon spp., 50

Apple serviceberry, *10*

Apricot, 30

Aquilegia spp., 58

Aster novae-angiae, 47

Bamboo, 18

Bambusa multiplex riviereorum, 18

Bambusa spp., 18

Bee balm, *15*, 28, 60

Berberis spp., 18, 19

Bidens aristosa, 47, 47

Bird behavior

       mating, 106–108

       nesting, 109–112

       migration, 117

Bird feeder, 32, 71–81, 82

       platform feeder, 75, *75*

       hopper feeder, 76, *76*

       tube feeder, 78, *78*

       suet cage, 78, *78*

       nectar feeder, 80, *80*

       fruit feeder, 81, *81*

       diversion feeder, 81

Birdbath heater, 70

Birdbath, 31, 68–71, *68*, *91*

Birdhouse, 14, *67*, 84–89

Blackberry, *34*, 53

Blazing star, *28*

Blue jay, *101*

Blue-gray gnatcatcher, *110*

Blueberry, 30, 53

Bluebird, 20

Bluestem, 50

Buddleia davidii, 59

Bullock's oriole, 116

Bushtit, 20

Butterfly bush, 59

Buxus spp., 18

Camellia japonica, 18

Campsis radicans, 59

Cardinal, *13*

Carolina chickadee, *114*

Carpinus betulus, 18

Catmint, 60

Cedar waxwing, *30*, *41*

Chaenomeles speciosa, 59

Chamaecyparis lawsoniana, 18

Cherry, 30, 52

Chimney swift, 20

Chive, 36

Cleome hasslerana, 59

Cleome, 59

Cocculus laurifolius, 18

Columbine, 58

Compact xylosma, 18

Companion planting, 24, 25

Compost, 21, 22

Coral bells, 60, *60*

Cornelian cherry, 19

Cornus florida, 51

Cornus mas, 19

Corylus avellana, 19

Cosmos bipinatus, 48, *48*

Cosmos, 48

Cotoneaster acutifolius, 19

Cotoneaster, 30

Crabapple, 19, 51, *51*

Crataegus spp., 19

Cupressocyparis leylandii, 18

Dark-eyed junco, *33*, *105*

Darwin barberry, 18

Delphinium spp., 59

Dicksissel, *92–93*

Eastern bluebird, *67*, *97*

Eastern meadowlark, *107*

Eastern white pine, 18

Echinacea purpurea, *28*, *44*, *48*, *48*

Elaeagnus pungens, 18

Elderberry, 30, 53

English boxwood, 18

English laurel cherry, 18

Eryngium, 36

Escallonia rubra, 18

Euonymus alata, 19

Euonymus fortunei, 18

European beech, 19

European hornbeam, 18

Evergreen euonymus, 18

Fagus sylvatica, 19

False holly, 18

Filbert, 19

Fir, 33

Firethorn, 18

Flowering dogwood, 51

Flowering quince, 59

Flowering tobacco, 61

Forsythia intermedia, 19

Forsythia, 19

Four o'clock, 60

Foxtail grass, 50

Fragraria spp., 51

Fraser photinia, 18

Fuchsia spp. 59

Geranium, 61

Glossy abelia, 18

Grape, wild, 54

Hand-feeding, 114

Hawthorn, 19

Heavenly bamboo, 18

Hedge cotoneaster, 19

Hedge maple, 19

Helianthus spp. *40–41* , 48

Hemlock, 33, 53

Heuchera spp. 60, *60*

Holly, 18, 30, 33, 51

House finch, *107*

Hummingbird sage, *46*

Hummingbirds, 42, 58

Hyssop, *58*

Ilex spp., 18, 33, 51

Impatiens wallerana, 60

Impatiens, 60

India hawthorn, 18

Indigo bunting, *73*

Insect spray, homemade, 20

Insecticidal soap, 21

Japanese barberry, 19

Japanese boxwood, 18

Japanese camellia, 18

Japanese pagoda tree, 19

Japanese privet, 18

Juniper, 18, 33

Juniperus spp. , 18, 33

Juniperus virginiana, 19

Kentucky warbler, *103*

Laurel-leaf cocculus, 18

Leyland cypress, 18

Liatrus spp., *28*

Ligustrum spp., 18, 19

Lilac, 19

Lonicera korolkowii 'Zabeli', *19*

Magellan barberry, 18

Mahonia aquifolium, 18

Malus spp., 19, 51, *51*

Maple, 50

Mentor barberry, 19

Milium, 50

Millet, 50

Mirabilis jalapa, 60

Mockingbird, 20

Monarda didyma, 60

Monarda spp., *15, 28*

Morus spp., 52

Mourning dove, *100*

Mulberry, 52

Myrtus communis, 18

Nandina domestica, 18

Narcissus, *26*

Nepeta spp., 60

Nest box, *85, 89*

Nesting, 34

New England aster, 47

Nicotiana spp., 61

Oregon grape, 18

Orioles, 20

Osmanthus heterophyllus, 18

Papaver, 36

Peach, 30

Pelargonium spp, 61

Pelargonium x *hortorum,* 61

Penstemon parryii, 16

Penstemon spp., 62

Petunia spp., 62

Phlox paniculata, 62

Phlox spp., *15, 36*, 62

Phoebe, 20

Photinia fraseri, 18

Picea spp., 33

Pine, 33

Pineapple sage, 63

Pinus strobus, 18

Pinus spp., 33

Plant hardiness zones, 46

Podocarpus macrophyllus, 18

Poppy, 36

Port Orford cedar, 18

Portugal laurel, 18

Privet, 18

Prunus laurocerasus, 18

Prunus lustanica, 18

Prunus spp. 52

Purple coneflower, *28*, 48, *48*

Purple finch, *104*

Pyracantha spp., 18, 30

Raspberry, 30, 53

Red-breasted nuthatch, 79

Red-headed woodpecker, 45

Red-winged blackbird, *73*

Rhaphiolepis indica, 18

Rhododendron spp. , 18

Rhododendron, 18

Rhus spp., 52

Rosa spp. 52

Rose, 52

Rose-breasted grosbeak, *102*

Rosehip, *43*

Rubus spp., 53

Ruby escallonia, 18

Rudbeckia spp. 49

Rufous hummingbird, *80*

Salmonella, and feeders, 77

Salvia elegans, 63

Salvia leucantha, 46

Salvia spp., 62

Sambucus spp., 53

Scented geraniums, 61

Serviceberry, 51

Shiny xylosma, 19

Silverberry, 18

Sophora japonica, 19

Sorghum bicolor, *50*

Sorghum, *50*

Spruce, 33

Squirrels, 82–83

Strawberry, wild, 30, 51

Suet, 78–79

Sumac, 30, 52

Sunflower, *40–41*, 48

Swallows, 20

Syringa spp., 19

Taxus spp., 18

Thuja spp., 18

Tickseed sunflower, 47, *47*

Tithonia rotundifolia, 49, *49*, 63

Tithonia, 49, *49* , 63

Tree swallow, *84*

True myrtle, 18

Trumpet vine, 30, 59

Tsuga spp., 33, 53

Tufted titmouse, *43*

Vaccinium spp., 53

Viburnum spp. , 18, 30, 54

Vicary golden privet, 19

Vitus spp., 54

Warbling vireos, 20

Western tanager, *95*

White-breasted nuthatch, *99*

Wilson's warbler, *96*

Winged burning bush, 19

Winter wren, *98*

Wrens, 20

Xylosma congestum 'Compacta', 18

Xylosma congestum, 19

Yellow warblers, 20

Yellowthroat, *93*

Yew pine, 18

Yew, 18

Yucca filamentosa, 49

Zabel's honeysuckle, 19

Zinnia, *17*, 49, *49*

PHOTO CREDITS